Football
Inside the Game

Chris Nawrat

Published in 1998 by Icon Books Ltd,
Grange Road, Duxford, Cambridge CB2 4QF
e-mail: icon@mistral.co.uk

Distributed in the UK, Europe, Canada, South Africa and Asia
by the Penguin Group:
Penguin Books Ltd, 27 Wrights Lane, London W8 5TZ

Published in Australia in 1998 by Allen & Unwin Pty Ltd,
PO Box 8500, 9 Atchison Street, St. Leonards, NSW 2065

ISBN 1 84046 028 8

Series edited by Sport and Leisure Books Ltd
Layout and illustrations: Zoran Jevtic, Audiografix
Cover design by Zoran Jevtic and Jeremy Cox
Photographs supplied by Colorsport

Printed and bound in Great Britain by
Biddles Ltd, Guildford and King's Lynn

CONTENTS

I dedicate this book to my late wife, Christine Boyle

All the World's a Stage

After the World Cup draw in December 1997, the *Independent* newspaper devoted its main editorial leader to the importance of football as a global, unifying force, claiming that 'football is the most powerful agent of modern internationalism'. At first sight this seems a somewhat extravagant statement, indeed even a hostage to fortune, burdening a mere sport at the end of the twentieth century with the responsibility of improving the world. But the *Independent* is not alone in believing that football is a cultural unifier.

Two years earlier, in the *Evening Standard*, Melvyn Bragg wrote: 'Football is one of the very few, perhaps now the only, subject on which it is possible to have an intelligent and equal conversation in this country across class, cash and colour.' Part of the reason for this multi-racial dimension to football in Europe is the large number of black players now in the game – in Britain the proportion of black players far outweighs that of the nation as whole – and the mobility of overseas players. In the Premiership there are over 150 foreigners plying their trade. In such a climate, racism and xenophobia wither rather than thrive.

The World Cup itself – indisputably the greatest show on earth – shrinks the globe as, every four years, virtually every country in the world embarks on a journey of dreams that they hope will take them to the World Cup finals. For the 1998 tournament, 174 nations entered the competition and 32 qualified for the finals. The television audience was measured in billions. Few events generate such interest and passion – the collapse of the Berlin Wall, perhaps, or the ending of apartheid – but football does it on a regular basis. Until recently, the Olympics was seen as the sporting event that unified the world. Now the World Cup finals dwarf the discredited and drug-riven Olympic games, generating twice as much revenue and supplanting it as the major sports occasion on earth.

The *Independent* described 'the beautiful game' as 'the only truly secular religion, providing a common culture for the world in the way Christendom and Latin once did for Europe'. There are, I think, two main reasons for this international fascination with football. First, it is very simple and second, it is essentially democratic. The basic rules of the game have hardly altered since 1926 and are absurdly easy to understand – children grasp them within seconds. And you do not have to be a particular shape or size – unlike, say, American gridiron football – to play the game. For example, Paul Gascoigne hardly fits the part as a consummate athlete – but he is. Centre-forwards can be tall, massive creatures such as Duncan Ferguson or midget-like bombshells like Michael Owen. Interestingly, it is for precisely these reasons that football is the most popular sport played by girls in the United States.

Also you do not need any expensive equipment to play the game – a ball and a playground or a park and you can play. The goalposts can be jackets thrown on the ground. A Gallup poll in 1998 indicated that football is played daily by 1.2 billion people – a fifth of the world's population. As you read this, youngsters in Africa, South America and Wandsworth Common are doing just that. On the sandy beaches outside São Paulo, there are hundreds of permanent goalposts for kids from the *favelas* (the shanty towns) to hone their skills. Little wonder that Brazil have won the World Cup four times, more than any other nation.

In essence, football is a game about creativity, the desire to score goals. Even defence is predicated on attack. When a defender wins the ball deep in his own half he is thinking of how he can get it to his forwards so they can score. Nobody ever won a game 0– 0, if we leave aside the aberration of penalty shoot-outs. Also it is a team game, a collective attempt by eleven players to impose their artistic and athletic will on eleven others. Inevitably there will be stars, players more gifted than others, but football is a supreme example of the whole being greater than the sum of its parts.

Other major spectator team sports pall in comparison. Cricket and baseball, for example, are two sports played with a ball where the accent is on containment, not creativity. When one side has the ball their intention is to destroy. If you like, their best form of attack is defence, to bowl the other side out. By the same token, the attack – the creative aspect of both sports – the scoring of runs can only be achieved by one man outwitting an entire team. In cricket, the draw is a prevalent result, and sometimes a moral victory. In baseball, according to Roger Angell (a prominent analyst): 'Losing rather than winning is what baseball is all about. If you can't cope with constant, unrelenting, inescapable failure, you just can't play baseball. It will eat you alive.' Some commentators have suggested that this says something profound about America, about the minuscule margin between failure and success: to survive you have to sacrifice.

Gridiron American football tells you something else about America. This is a ball game with a difference. Here the attack and defence are two different teams. They don't even play on the field at the same time. An American football team is a team like an electrician and a plumber: you need both to make your central heating system work, but they can't do each other's job. Unlike its small-ball cousin, American football is based on a more hard-nosed capitalist ethos: you get four opportunities to achieve your target; if you succeed you get another four opportunities and so on, until you achieve your goal. If you screw up, the other side gets your chance. Little wonder that American football with its late-twentieth-century capitalist philosophy and in an age where television is king, displaced baseball, with its more pre-war sacrifice-to-survive ideology, as America's No 1 sport in the 1970s.

So if the two leading American sports can be seen as cultural indexes of their economic and political philosophies, what do we make of professional football, born as it was in the nineteenth century in public schools and then wrested away by the working class and re-forged in the heartland of industrial England? Perhaps this is one of the key secrets in football's worldwide appeal: perhaps England accidentally forged a sport from its working-class heritage that epitomised social democracy, a sport that was egalitarian and collective, a sport that would endure, thrive, and take us into the twenty-first century.

But its liberal origins do not fully explain the global fascination with watching the game. All sport can claim to be unscripted theatre, but most have flaws that narrow their appeal. Cricket takes too long and the lbw rule is arcane; much of what happens in rugby takes place in the hidden battles of scrums and mauls; golf is a good walk spoilt; boxing is legalised brutality; men's tennis is a blur – women's, metronomic. Only football provides pure, uncluttered and straightforward competition. The object of the game is simplicity itself: score more goals than the other guys.

As unscripted theatre, we expect from a football match what we would expect from a play. It must have a beginning, a middle and an end, in a fixed period of time. It must be entertaining and dramatic. It must have a meaning. It needs a good cast of characters all performing their roles to the best of their ability. But what draws us to the pitch rather than the stage is the absence of a script and the feverish anticipation of the outcome. We do not know what is going to happen. But we care, and we know that we may not see the result we would wish. We may not even see an entertaining match.

The hero: Joe Baker in the 'hated' Arsenal shirt

Therein lies the beauty. We will watch bad matches; our hopes for our team may be dashed; but we know we will also see some pulsating, heart-stopping games, joyous games that will live in the memory long after the final whistle.

As a thirteen-year-old schoolboy, I was taken to see Torino play Napoli in the Italian Cup in 1962. Denis Law and Joe Baker were playing for Torino that day. I'd always been fascinated by Joe Baker, even though I'd never seen him play. That was because he was a centre-forward with the Edinburgh club, Hibernian, but, despite being Scottish-based, Baker had played for England. To my mind that was exotic. My school had connections with the Italian club and I was one of a bunch of English schoolkids privileged to get into the Torino dressing-room after the game (which Torino lost). I was permitted to put on the shirt that Denis Law had worn in the match and talk to Joe Baker. I was star-struck, but not tongue-tied. I asked my idol which English club he wanted to play for (there was much speculation about his return to British football) and Baker said Tottenham. This was my team. The bond became rock-solid.

In the event, he went to the hated Arsenal. I swallowed hard and forgave him. Almost a decade later, I was a student at Edinburgh University and had little choice but to adopt Hibs as my Scottish club. Hibs had begun the season badly and there was a stream of stories in the press saying that Baker would be returning to his old stamping ground. Baker had now turned thirty, and was languishing at Sunderland, having first moved to Nottingham Forest from Arsenal. In the Leith pubs there was only one topic of conversation. And then he signed. There was one, small problem. Hibs' next opponents were Aberdeen, who had begun the season like a train and had yet to concede a goal, let alone lose a match. The ground was packed and I was in the middle of the high, sloping terrace at Easter Road when the great man appeared in his No 9 shirt. The ground buzzed with anticipation. And he did it, he really did. He scored twice in the first half. The roar when he put the first one in was the most extraordinary sound I'd heard. Like a gasp that becomes a shout. The whisky bottles were passed up and down the terrace as complete strangers hugged each other and tears of joy streamed down our faces. The same thing happened when he repeated the feat. Hibernian won and we all went home with lumps in our throats.

Every football fan has a story, or stories, like that to tell. It's the reason we watch football. Not even William Shakespeare could move me the way I was moved that day. Watching football is not a neutral activity. You support a team – for whatever reason – and indulge in partisan participation. Some supporters inherit a team from their family and are stuck with it for life, whether that team is successful or fashionable. Others inherit their allegiance from their community, and the connection between supporter and local club creates a bond that no civic initiative could ever enjoy. In The Fantasy chapter, I have written about Blackburn Rovers to attempt to illustrate this phenomenon.

Part of the purpose of this book is to address readers who feel much the same about the game as I do, who are also caught in a life-long, monogamous love affair with the beautiful game. Another is to explain to those who have only recently begun following the game avidly what exactly it is that goes on out there on those hallowed turfs. Yet another is to share those insights I have picked up over the decades and get behind the match reports we devour so eagerly in our newspapers.

Football's history is rich and colourful and is more than just a collection of results and league tables. I have sought to take a critical review of football in the twentieth century and have done my best to provide insights into how the modern game is played, how it got there, where it is going and to unravel the various systems that modernity has imposed on the structure and strategies of team play. I have endeavoured to make them transparent and improve your enjoyment of watching the greatest game on earth.

I need to acknowledge a number of people who were crucial to this book. Rab MacWilliam, whose idea it was and who talked me into it; Julia Casterton, a woman I love greatly, who put up with interminable conversations about the text, even though, in reality, it bored her stiff. As a Nottingham Forest supporter who stood on the terraces through the dark days before Brian Clough, and later became a poet and a tutor in creative writing, Julia was ever quick to pick up on my clumsy phrasing and cliched writing. (I'm not sure she caught all of it.) And Brian Glanville, a football journalist who tutored me with his perceptive writing on the *Sunday Times* throughout the 1960s and 1970s. In the 1980s and 1990s I was privileged to work with him. Serious football journalism owes Brian a lot.

Garth Crooks was another friend I leant on greatly. As a player and a figure inside the game, he achieved it all. From FA Cups to the PFA Chairmanship to football journalism. I owe him an enormous debt of gratitude, but any errors that have crept into the text are entirely my own. Julia is also completely blameless.

• The game starts with a kick-off. The team who win the toss choose ends. The ball is placed on the centre-spot and kicked by a player who may not play the ball again until another player has touched it. The ball must travel forwards and, if the player kicking off wishes, he may attempt to score a goal direct from the kick-off. Both teams must only occupy their own half of the field and none of the opposing players should be within ten yards of the centre-spot. The game also re-starts with a kick-off after a goal is scored – when the team conceding the goal re-start the match – and to start the second half, where both teams have changed ends. The team which did not start the match take the kick-off for the second half.

• The referee is responsible for monitoring the amount of time played and will add on more time to the ninety minutes duration to compensate for stoppages, or time-wasting. When ninety minutes are completed, he will signal, in some competitions, how many more minutes the game has to go. If a penalty is awarded just as the half is due to finish, the referee will allow the kick to be taken and a goal awarded even though the half is officially over. However, if the goalkeeper parries the penalty-kick, and the penalty-taker, or any other player, puts the ball in the net, it will not count as a goal.

• The referee does not necessarily have to award a free-kick or a penalty when a player has infringed the Laws of the Game. He may decide to play 'advantage' by allowing play to continue if, in his opinion, the attacking team would benefit. If the referee does allow 'advantage' this does not prevent him eventually booking – or sending off – the offending player. He will do so when the ball next goes out of play.

• At penalty-kicks – only the penalty-taker and the goalkeeper are allowed inside the penalty area – if a player from either side enters the area before the kick is taken, the kick will normally be re-taken. However, if the encroachment is from the defending side, or both teams together, and the ball has entered the net, a goal will be given. If the ball rebounds from the woodwork, without the goalkeeper or another player touching it, the penalty-taker cannot shoot again, but a teammate can.

• Other than a kick-off, the match is re-started in one of five different ways: a free-kick; a corner-kick; a goal-kick; a throw-in; and a dropped ball.

• There are two types of free-kick – direct and indirect. For a more detailed discussion see page 44.

• A corner is awarded when the defending team play the ball over the goal-line – other than into the net – and is taken from that corner of the field nearest the point at which the ball crossed the line. Once an attacking player has taken a corner-kick, he may not touch the ball again until it has touched another player. A goal can be scored direct from a corner-kick.

• A goal-kick is awarded when the attacking team play the ball over the goal-line – other than into the net – and is taken from anywhere inside the goal area and by any member of the defending team. The ball has to pass outside the area before another player can play it. If a player from either side plays the ball before it has left the area, the kick must be re-taken. A goal cannot be scored direct from a goal-kick.

• A throw-in is awarded when the ball has crossed either touchline. A player from the team that did not put the ball over the line takes the throw from where the incident occurred. He takes the ball in both of his hands – this is the only time that an outfield player can legally use his hands – and, with both feet on the ground, either on or behind the touchline, takes the ball behind his head and throws it into play. The player taking the throw-in must not play the ball again until it has touched another player. If he commits any infringement, the throw-in reverts to the other side.

• A dropped ball is an unusual occurrence in modern football. It is often employed when the referee wants to halt play so that an injured player can be treated. However, nowadays most professionals deliberately kick the ball out of play to stop the game when a player is down with an injury. (The unwritten code of the game is that possession is returned to the team that kicked the ball out.) After a referee has stopped the game, he re-starts it at the point where it was stopped by dropping the ball between two opposing players. No player can touch the ball until it has bounced.

• For the purposes of the Laws of the Game, the referee is regarded as 'part of the furniture of football' in much the same way as goalposts or corner flags. This means that he is not a 'player'. Therefore, in those situations where it is necessary for the ball to be touched by another player, the accident of the ball hitting the referee does not mean that the ball is in play.

• The referee has two assistants (formerly called linesmen) who run the touchlines for him, monitoring when the ball goes out of play, indicating offside positions and spotting any infringements that the referee has missed. They signal to the referee by raising a flag. This indicates which team should be given a throw-in, or whether a goal-kick or a corner should be awarded. The raising of a flag during open play also indicates offside. The two assistant referees run only one half of the field, diagonally opposite to each other.

• For a goal to be scored, the whole of the ball must cross the line. (The most famous example of this was England's third goal against West Germany in the 1966 World Cup final. Television replays have never fully settled the controversy, although the Germans are convinced it wasn't a goal. The issue still rankles, so much so that, whenever a similar incident occurs, the German commentators call it a 'Wembleytor'. *Tor* is German for goal.) An own goal cannot be conceded by a team taking a free-kick or a goal-kick. Instead, a corner to the defending side is awarded.

Dimensions of the goal: 8 yards wide, 8 feet high.

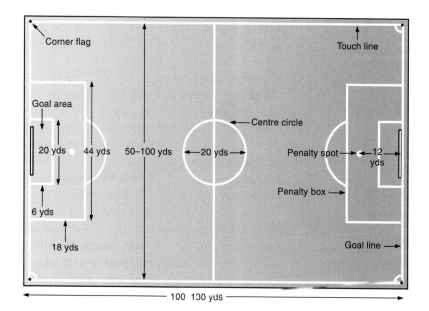

1863 Formation of the Football Association

1871 Birth of the FA Cup

1872 Wanderers beat the Royal Engineers 1–0 at the Oval to win the inaugural FA Cup in front of 20,000 spectators

1872 First international fixture between England in Scotland ends in 0–0 draw in Glasgow

1873 Birth of the Scottish FA Cup

1874 Queen's Park beat Clydesdale 2–0 to win the first Scottish Cup

1882 The English, Scottish, Welsh and Irish associations formed the International Football Association Board as the guardian of the rules

1885 The FA agreed to allow professionalism

1885 Arbroath beat Bon Accord 36–0 in the Scottish Cup. It is still a record for an official match. On the same day Dundee Harps beat Aberdeen Rovers 35–0

1888 The Football League was formed with twelve clubs from the North and Midlands

Virtually any country in the world with a history to speak of can claim that they invented football. Whether it was the Chinese in the Th'ng Dynasty, the ancient Greeks or Romans, the Mexicans, the Italians, Saxon peasants in mediaeval times ... every culture (with the notable exception of America) has tried to claim a piece of the football historical pie. No matter. The fact is that young males played something with something resembling a ball and that this is a global phenomenon going back to the dawn of time.

However, certain facts are undisputed and incontrovertible. The oldest international football fixture is England versus Scotland (born 1872); the oldest football association is the FA (born 1863); the oldest competition is the FA Cup (born 1872); and the oldest league is the Football League (born 1888). Professionalism was also first accepted in English football in 1885. The rules of the game, which by and large are still the same today, were formulated by the fledgling FA. Scotland soon followed England's lead, and it was these two nations that gave the game to the world.

By 1882, Ireland and Wales had joined the fold, and the four Home countries met in Manchester, unified their rules and, presumptuously, called themselves the International Football Association Board, and therefore the guardian of the rules of the game. Amazingly, these four tiny countries still have similar powers today, despite the fact that nearly 200 countries have football associations. The arrogance of the British in the first part of the twentieth century was to prove costly, as their insularity caused them to spend a half-century in self-imposed exile from the rest of the world.

The growth of football in Europe was exponential. By 1903, a number of countries, notably France, were battering at the FA's door demanding that a worldwide umbrella organisation be formed. The FA dithered, dallied and stonewalled. Fed up with this inertia, France unilaterally established Fifa in Paris in 1904 along with Belgium, Denmark, Holland, Spain, Sweden and Switzerland. Belatedly, the FA joined Fifa (sort of), but an arcane row over semi-professionalism in the 1928 Olympics gave the four Home countries the excuse they wanted to quit Fifa and enjoy their splendid isolation.

Thus it was that the inaugural World Cup of 1930, and the World Cups of 1934 and 1938, took place without any British involvement whatsoever. England and Scotland steadfastly believed that their annual fixture was the championship of the world and anything else was a sideshow. England did deign to play Italy, the newly crowned world champions, in London in 1934. The confrontation was not so much a football match, as a pitched battle. England, fielding seven Arsenal players on their home ground, prevailed 3–2. With Arsenal's Ted Drake leading the line, the jingoistic press portrayed the encounter as Drake's Armada doing battle with Mussolini's army. Their wish was fulfilled and the skirmish became known as the Battle of Highbury, with noses broken, legs fractured and numerous players leaving the field battered and bruised.

But England won, so they were still the real champions of the world – weren't they? This nonsense persisted until after the Second World War when the four Home Countries were finally persuaded to re-join Fifa and enter the 1950 World Cup. Generously, Fifa designated the Home championships as a World Cup qualifying group

1889 Preston North End won the first championship without losing a game and completed the Double by winning the FA Cup without conceding a goal

1890 Scottish Football League formed with eleven clubs

1891 Dumbarton and Rangers joint winners of the first Scottish championship

1892 Football League created a Second Division

1893 Scottish FA agreed to allow professionalism

1897 Aston Villa became the second club to win the Double of League and FA Cup

1901 Southern League Tottenham win the FA Cup by beating Sheffield United 3–1 after a replay. Tottenham are the only non-League team to have achieved this feat

1902 Terracing collapsed at Ibrox at the start of the annual Scotland-England match. Twenty-five people died and more than 500 were injured

with the top two eligible for the finals. However, despite the cessation of hostilities, Scotland decided to play the Colonel Blimp card and announced they would not go to the finals in Brazil unless they were the British champions. The Scots' come-uppance came when they lost 1–0 to England at Hampden Park and surrendered the Home championship. Stubborn to a fault, they refused to go, despite the protestations of their players and pleas from the English. Perhaps it was the right decision. England lost unceremoniously 1–0 to the rag, tag and bobtail United States and did their international reputation no good whatsoever.

Such was the rough-and-tumble debut of the two founding fathers of world football into the real world. But it would take decades before they acclimatised; and there were still more painful lessons to be learnt by the self-proclaimed masters of the universe.

Learning the Hard Way – 1950 to 1970

England regarded their defeat at the hands of the American bit-players in 1950 as just a blip, as they did their defeat by the Republic of Ireland in Liverpool in 1949 – their first home international defeat by non-British opposition. The Irish team were composed of nine players from the Football League. The USA side also had Football League exiles in it. So, to England's way of thinking, neither result really counted. In 1953, England's cosy little belief that they were simply the best was smashed to smithereens. The Hungarians breezed into London and demolished England 6–3, then, six months later, repeated the exercise with a 7–1 thrashing in Budapest.

The modernisation of the British game was

1904 Fifa was formed in Paris with seven European countries present. England, Scotland, Wales and Ireland declined to take part

1904 Arsenal won promotion to the First Division, the first Southern club to do so

1905 The Mears family unveiled 100,000-capacity Stamford Bridge stadium. And then decided to create Chelsea FC

1905 Alf Common became the first £1,000 transfer when he moved to Middlesbrough from Sunderland

1906 The FA reluctantly joined Fifa, but Scotland and Ireland were excluded because of suspicions about their close ties with the FA

1906 Argentina and Uruguay played the first South American international match

1907 Celtic became the first club to win the Scottish Double and repeated the feat the following year

1908 Players' Union officially formed

underway, but the domestic culture of insularity and backwardness still prevailed. When floodlights were first introduced in Britain in 1952, they were banned by a blinkered FA. The harbingers of doom warned that they would be the death-knell of football. Arsenal and Rangers installed them anyway, but it was three years before they were permitted in competitive matches. And when the European Cup was launched in 1955, Chelsea, the League champions, were 'persuaded' by the Football League not to enter. The justification for this advice was that Chelsea would find it difficult to fulfil the extra fixtures. So, just like the inaugural World Cup in 1930, England once again stubbornly refused to participate in the birth of an epoch-changing competition. The authorities saw no need for change, and therefore saw a need not to change.

After all, the League championship and FA Cup were flourishing with some fine teams in the 1950s. The Stanley Matthews final, when the thirty-eight-year-old winger had inspired Blackpool to come back from 3–1 down to beat Bolton 4–3 with two goals in the last three minutes, enthralled the nation in Coronation year. Jackie Milburn's Newcastle became the first team to win back-to-back Cup finals this century in 1951 and 1952. Wolves won the League title three times and impressively beat Continental club opposition in friendlies – including the Hungarians. Matt Busby's Babes were blossoming at Manchester United. To many eyes, everything in the garden was rosy.

There were visionaries, however. When Manchester United won the Football League championship in 1956, Busby spurned the League's 'advice' and agreed to take part in the European Cup. 'The Continental challenge should be met, not avoided',

1909 More than 100 people were injured when angry spectators rioted after the Scottish Cup final replay between Rangers and Celtic ended in another draw. Believing that the two draws had been stage-managed to bring in extra gate money, the crowd used whisky to try to burn down the stand. The Cup was withheld

1909 Newcastle won the First Division title despite losing 9–1 at home to Sunderland

1915 Four Liverpool and four Manchester United players were banned for life for rigging their match in a betting coup

1919 Despite only finishing sixth in the Second Division, Arsenal were voted into the First Division when it expanded from twenty clubs to twenty-two. To date, Arsenal have never been relegated

1920 The League formed the Third Division and, a year later, divided it into two, North and South. This virtually doubled the size of the League in two seasons

the Manchester United manager said. They reached the semi-finals, losing to Real Madrid, the holders and eventual winners. The Spanish champions won the first five European Cups and dazzled all of Europe with their skills and artistry. Whether that Busby team would ever have reached Real's dizzying heights we will never know. The air crash in Munich in 1958 when the team were returning from a European Cup-tie against Red Star Belgrade ripped the heart out of the side when eight of the team, including the incomparable Duncan Edwards, were killed. Wolves won the championship that year and entered the European Cup. As a mark of respect for United's tragic loss, Uefa offered Manchester United a place as well. Curmudgeons to a man, the Football League refused them permission. Busby had never been forgiven for snubbing their 'advice' in 1956.

Ten years after the Munich air crash, another Manchester United team exorcised the ghosts for Busby, becoming the first English club to lift the European Cup when they beat Benfica 4–1 after extra time at Wembley. An Irish imp called George Best scored the goal that broke the Portuguese club's spirits three minutes into the extra period. Jock Stein's Celtic had snapped the Continental grip on the trophy the year before, when they had prised open the tight oyster of Helenio Herrera's ultra-defensive Inter Milan and beaten them 2–1 in Lisbon, helped by a pearl of a goal from Tommy Gemmell.

England and, occasionally, Scotland continued to qualify for the World Cup finals, but without making any impression. England tended to reach the quarter-finals (or a play-off for the quarter-finals) before being eliminated. Scotland only drew one match in their first two tournaments and failed

---

1923 The first FA Cup final at the newly-opened Wembley stadium was a near-disaster, as over a quarter of million people descended on the 127,000-capacity ground and forced their way in. Mounted police dispersed the crowd that spilled on to the pitch. One PC, in particular, was most evident because his horse, Billy, was white. Inevitably, it is remembered as the White Horse final

1923 Southampton had the perfect average season: P 42, Pts 42, W 14, D 14, L 14

1924 Newcastle beat Aston Villa 2–0 to win the FA Cup at Wembley. It ended an amazing sequence. Newcastle had played in the final five times between 1905 and 1911 at Crystal Palace, the final's previous venue, and had never won there

1924 Huddersfield pipped Cardiff to the League title on goal average by 0.0241 of a goal. If goal difference had been used instead, Cardiff would have been champions

to qualify in 1962, 1966 and 1970. Instead, it was Brazil and Pele that were setting the new agenda, winning the 1958, 1962 and 1970 World Cups in exhilarating style. The appointment of Alf Ramsey as the England manager in 1963 was a significant move towards a more professional approach to international football. Ramsey, a former England player, took it further than the FA may have envisaged. He promptly announced that he would select the team. Hitherto it had been chosen by committee. Then he announced to the press that England would definitely win the next World Cup. He was as good as his word. In 1966, England took full advantage of hosting the tournament and, by the 1970 World Cup finals in Mexico, the World Cup holders were ranked alongside Brazil as one of the two best international teams in the world.

Glory Nights in Europe – 1960 to 1985

Once the European citadel had been breached, British clubs flooded across the Channel in search of booty and, from 1977 to 1982, English clubs won six straight European Cup finals. But it was a slow learning curve. In 1963, Tottenham were the first British team to win a European trophy, when Danny Blanchflower's fabulous Double team (plus Jimmy Greaves) swept aside the holders, Atletico Madrid, 5–1 in the European Cup Winners Cup in Rotterdam. Rangers had lost a two-legged final in the same competition two years earlier. However, the European Cup Winners Cup was hardly the European Cup. It was a relatively new competition and, in virtually all Continental countries, their domestic Cup competitions were (and still are) very much small beer compared to the League championship. It was viewed abroad as a competition for also-rans.

1925 The offside rule was changed so that it only needed two men, instead of three, to be between an attacking player and the goal when the ball was passed for the play to be onside

1926 Manchester City became the first team to lose the Cup final and be relegated in the same season

1926 The change in the offside rule created a goal bonanza with 6,373 scored in the League as compared with 4,700 the year before

1927 The FA Cup left England for the first time when Cardiff beat Arsenal 1–0 because of a blunder by Arsenal's Welsh goalkeeper

1928 Everton's Dixie Dean broke the League's goal-scoring record – set by Middlesbrough's George Camsell with fifty-nine the year before – with a hat-trick in the final match of the season to take his tally to sixty

1928 The four British associations quit Fifa over a row about payments at the Olympics

1929 England suffered their first defeat by Continental opponents when they lost 4–3 to Spain in Madrid

1930 The first World Cup took place in Uruguay and the host nation beat Argentina 4–2 in the final. None of the four British countries took part

1933 Third Division Walsall, whose team had cost £69, knocked mighty Arsenal, who had cost over £30,000, out of the FA Cup, 2–0

1934 The second World Cup was won by the host nation, Italy. They beat Czechoslovakia 2–1 after extra time

1935 Arsenal won their third championship in a row to emulate Huddersfield's record in the 1920s. Herbert Chapman, who had died suddenly the previous season, was the manager who had guided both teams

Still, it was a beginning, and British clubs built on Tottenham's modest incursion. Two years later, West Ham won the self-same trophy and Liverpool and Rangers were losing finalists in the years following. Indeed, Rangers' place in that final completed a special British treble, as Celtic won the European Cup and Leeds lost in the third European competition, the Fairs Cup (later renamed the Uefa Cup). The bandwagon was definitely rolling, with Manchester United taking the European Cup the following year and Leeds also winning the Fairs Cup. Leeds' victory began a roll of five more successive English victories in the Fairs Cup/Uefa Cup, until Spurs lost the 1974 final. Much the same was true in the Cup Winners Cup. Manchester City were the victors in 1970, Chelsea and Rangers followed and the run ended in 1973, when Leeds lost in the final.

The success stories seemed never-ending. But the stranglehold British clubs had on the lesser two competitions in the late 1960s and early 1970s was only a chimerical European triumph. British clubs had stormed through the gates, but couldn't lay their hands on the crown jewels. In the eight European Cup finals since Manchester United had conquered Europe's citadel, only two British clubs had reached the final, Celtic in 1970 and Leeds in 1975. Both lost. British clubs basked in their European triumphs, and pundits used them to argue that 'we' were as good as the cream of the Continent. It was not true.

It was an honest mistake. In the 1960s and 1970s, Europe and its Leagues were still largely a mystery to the average English fan. He would have assumed that they would be much the same as in England with a significant number of clubs jostling for the championship and a prestigious Cup competition that had more glamour than the League title. This is only true in England. The main Continental football-playing nations of Germany, Holland, Italy, Portugal and Spain are generally dominated by an elite of two or three clubs. For this elite there are only two competitions worth a toss: their championship and the European Cup. Everything else is dross. That is why Bobby Robson can win the European Cup Winners Cup, the Spanish Cup and finish runner-up in the League in his first season with Barcelona and be removed as the coach. Of the sixty-six Spanish League titles contested, Barcelona and Real Madrid have won forty-one of them and only six other clubs have ever won it at all.

Much the same is true in other European countries – not least Scotland. This hegemony by an elite in each country, and their attitude to what success really is, is amply demonstrated in the first twenty-one years of the European Cup. Apart from the exceptions of Celtic and Manchester United, only 5 countries had won Europe's biggest club prize in that period: Spain (6), Holland (4), Italy (4), Germany (3) and Portugal (2). And of those 19 victories, they were shared among a mere 7 clubs: Real Madrid with 6, Ajax (3), Bayern (3), Benfica (2), Inter (2), Milan (2) and Feyenoord (1).

The traditional English disdain for ball skills, tactics and technical skills also played into the hands of their more sophisticated Continental opponents. Bill Shankly, a colossus of a manager with Liverpool, was a pygmy when it came to Europe. He was naturally xenophobic and hated their football and their tactics. It wasn't until his successor, Bob Paisley, took over in 1974, that

1935 Fielding seven Arsenal players, England beat the newly-crowned world champions, Italy, 3–2, in a bad-tempered match that came to be known as the Battle of Highbury

1936 The first match to be shown on television was film of Arsenal v Everton

1938 The England team were ordered by the British embassy to give the Nazi salute on the field in a friendly international against Germany in Berlin and duly complied. Aston Villa, told to do the same thing the next day, refused

1938 East Fife became the first Second Division side to win the Scottish Cup beating First Division Kilmarnock 4–2 after extra time in a replay

Liverpool truly blossomed in Europe. The difficulty that English sides had was that the qualities required to win the championship were not those that would easily translate to the wily ways of the European Cup. Relying on speed, stamina and muscularity would get you through the slog of a forty-two-match marathon. But a home-and-away Cup competition on foreign fields was an entirely different proposition. What Paisley did was to develop a style that was suited to both. His phenomenal record – three European Cups, three Cup Winners Cups, one Uefa Cup, six League titles and three League Cups in nine seasons – more than proves he achieved it. In spades.

The Dark Days of English Football – 1974 to 1989

Hooliganism, of some kind, has swirled around the game since its inception. However nobody paid too much attention to it until the 1970s when it seemed to threaten to engulf the English game. Rotterdam, 21 May 1974, was a watershed. It wasn't the day hooliganism started, but it was an evening that brought shame to English football and its supporters and marked the birth of a new trend, the exportation of English hooliganism to foreign shores. Tottenham were playing Feyenoord in the first leg of the Uefa Cup final and, for no obvious reason, a number of their 'fans' created a riot in the stadium early in the match. Over 200 people were injured and 70 arrests were made. A year later, Leeds 'fans' repeated the exercise in Paris in the European Cup final against Bayern Munich. Their battle with the French riot police at least stemmed from perceived injustice on the field, but it was another night of shame for English football. Leeds were

1938 Italy, the defending champions, won the third World Cup in France when they beat Hungary 4–2 in the final

1938 The FA Cup final was the first full match to be shown live on television

1939 The League season was abandoned after three games when War broke out

1945 The four British associations re-joined Fifa

1946 Scottish League Cup created

1946 Crush barriers collapsed when over 85,000 people attempted to get in to see Bolton's second round FA Cup-tie with Stoke. In the mêlée, 33 people died and over 500 were injured

1946 The government banned midweek afternoon matches because they feared the game's postwar boom in popularity would lead to absenteeism

banned from European competition for four years. It made little difference. The cancer had taken hold.

And no matter what solution was proposed – from the birch to flame-throwers to identity cards – the problem would not go away. When Scottish fans ran amok on the pitch at Wembley in 1977 after their first victory over England on English soil for thirty-nine years, destroying both goals and carving out pieces of the turf to take home as souvenirs, fences were introduced. This became the way the game dealt with hooligans: cage them in. Despite liberal voices pleading that 'if you treat them like animals, they will behave like animals', fencing proliferated. At one point, Ken Bates, the Chelsea chairman, attempted to electrify his fences. Madness had bred madness and football hooliganism became so commonplace that it was just seen as one of the unwelcome ills of the sport. Not surprisingly, attendances slumped, as ordinary supporters feared for their safety. In 1981, 2.7 million fewer people had attended matches than the previous season. Worse was to come.

Travelling England supporters had already thrown down their gauntlet to Johnny Foreigner in 1977, when they attempted to wreck Luxembourg, and again in 1980, when they fought with Italians on the terraces in Turin during the European championships. It required batons and tear gas to break up the riot. The violence was escalating. In the 1981–2 season two fans were stabbed to death. Luxembourg was wrecked again in 1983, despite the deployment of police forces from four different countries. Then, in 1985, the roof finally caved in.

In March, hundreds of Millwall 'fans' engaged in a full-scale battle with over 200 police on Luton's

1946 For the first time in an FA Cup final, the ball burst as Derby beat Charlton 4–1. It happened again the next year when Charlton beat Burnley 1–0

1946 Nearly a million people went to the forty-three matches on the opening day of the first League season since the Second World War ended

1948 Manchester United's 4–2 FA Cup final defeat of Blackpool was watched by over one million people live on BBC television

1948 League attendances topped forty million for the first time

1949 Rangers became the first team to win the Treble of League, Scottish Cup and Scottish League Cup

pitch during an FA Cup-tie. They ripped up plastic seats, hurling them on to the pitch and using them as weapons and shields against the police. After the riot had subsided, the mob rampaged through the town, damaging shops, houses and cars before laying waste to the train back to London. The match was televised live and caused horror around the world. Forty-seven people, including thirty-one policemen, were injured. Government and football met to hammer out solutions to the growing problem, but the discussions got nowhere. The sale of alcohol was banned from football grounds and a national identity card scheme mooted.

While hooliganism was extensively reported, and endlessly discussed, another timebomb – the state of stadiums – was completely ignored. Two months after the Millwall riot, the timebomb went off, when a fire started in a wooden stadium at Bradford City and fifty-six people died in the inferno, with hundreds more suffering burns. It was the worst sporting disaster to occur in England. The tragedy highlighted how outdated and unsafe many stadiums were. The fire was caused by accumulated rubbish under the seventy-six-year-old stand being accidentally set alight. Fortunately for unfashionable, Third Division Bradford, they had had few problems with hooliganism and therefore had not fenced in their wooden stand. If they had done, the loss of life would have been far worse: the spectators who survived did so by scrambling on to the open pitch. However, eighteen days later the combination of a dilapidated stadium and hooliganism would be even more shocking.

The Heysel stadium in Brussels should never have been chosen as the venue for the European Cup final between Juventus and Liverpool. It was a

1949 The entire Torino squad – including eight Italian internationals – died when their plane crashed near Superga

1949 England lost their first match to non-British opposition when the Republic of Ireland beat them 1–0 at Goodison Park

1950 England's debut in the World Cup in Brazil was less than successful, as they embarrassingly lost 1–0 to the USA and won only one of their three matches. Scotland, piqued at not winning the British championship, refused to participate

1951 £100,000 was won on the pools for the first time

1952 Newcastle became the first team to retain the FA Cup since 1891 when they beat Arsenal 1–0

crumbling, ancient monstrosity and the Belgian authorities were incapable of organising such a highly-charged occasion. Security and policing were poor. There was no control over the sale of tickets, nor were there any attempts to check that spectators had not brought alcohol or weapons into the stadium. There was no closed circuit television and the emergency services on hand were ill-equipped to deal with a major crisis. On top of all that, Z section, designated as a neutral area for supporters, was an obvious death-trap, with no clear means of exit in an emergency. Carelessly, Italian fans were allowed to acquire tickets for the Z section, which was adjacent to the X and Y terraces restricted to Liverpool supporters. The Belgian police had not even anticipated that there might be violence before the kick-off and were caught completely off-guard.

The tragedy began when Juventus fans started taunting the Liverpool fans in the X and Y sections well before the kick-off, and escalated when the Liverpool fans broke into Z section and charged the Italians. Eight policemen looked on, doing nothing. The Liverpool fans charged twice more in the next half-hour, the third time with stones, beer cans, fists and fireworks. The Juventus fans attempted to run to safety, but in their panic they fell over each other as an old wall collapsed. People were crushed to death. When the police did intervene, they made matters worse by hitting the panic-stricken fans with batons, while others lay dying around them. In total, thirty-nine people died, all of them Italian. It was a desperate day for football and, shamefully, the match went ahead anyway. Uefa's response was swift and, understandably, heavy-handed: all English clubs were banned from European competitions indefinitely.

1952 The FA refused to allow clubs to use floodlights, but clubs experimented with them in friendly matches

1952 Neither Rangers nor Celtic won a major trophy. This had never happened before

1953 The amateur team, Walthamstow Avenue, reached the fourth round of the FA Cup and managed to draw with Manchester United at Old Trafford before losing the replay 5–2

1953 Charlie Tully scored direct from a corner for Celtic against Falkirk in the Scottish Cup but the goal was disallowed because the crowd had encroached on to the pitch and the kick had to be re-taken. And Tully duly did it again

This decision was not designed to solve the hooligan problem, but to confine the thugs to England. It did not deter them from following the national side abroad, where they continued to wreak mayhem, but it was a significant warning-shot across the bows of English football. It made little difference. It required another disaster, the worst in British sport, before football was finally forced to put its house in order.

Although hooliganism per se wasn't responsible for the Hillsborough tragedy in 1989, the reason why ninety-five spectators died at the FA Cup semi-final between Liverpool and Nottingham Forest was because they were fenced in. Those fences were only there because of the hooligan threat. When thousands of Liverpool fans, many of them ticketless, anxious to get into the Leppings Lanes end for the kick-off, surged through the gates, spectators were crushed by the perimeter fencing behind the Liverpool goal. Like Heysel, four years earlier, all the authorities had let the paying customers down. The ticket allocation was unbalanced. Liverpool, with an average home attendance of 40,000, had been given 24,000 tickets. Forest, with an average attendance of 17,000 had received 30,000. The police panicked and opened the gates when they shouldn't because of the number of people trying to get in to a confined space. The emergency services, ambulances and medical equipment were late in coming because they were not fully aware of the severity of the situation.

Lord Justice Taylor was commissioned to conduct an inquiry into the disaster and produced a damning report on the state of English football stadiums. Pointing out this was the ninth report on safety this century, he roundly condemned football's inactivity

1953 Stanley Matthews, at thirty-eight, finally collected his FA Cup-winner's medal when Blackpool beat Bolton 4–3 in one of the most dramatic finals. Blackpool, inspired by Matthews, recovered from being 3–1 down with twenty-two minutes remaining. Despite the fact that Stan Mortensen scored a hat-trick, it is known as the 'Matthews Final'

1953 England lost 6–3 to Hungary at Wembley. It was their first home defeat by Continental opposition. Six months later they lost 7–1 in Budapest

1954 Uefa was formed

1954 West Germany surprisingly won the World Cup by beating Hungary 3–2 in the final. It was the only match Hungary lost between 1950 and 1956

and the attitudes to ground safety. From now on football stadiums would have to be all-seated, the fences would disappear and closed circuit television introduced to combat hooliganism. And, despite some bleating, football accepted the recommendations and carried them out. Their resolution to do so was given greater impetus when Uefa, who had readmitted English clubs in 1990, decided that only clubs with all-seater stadiums could take part in their European competitions. And, by and large, the Taylor report has worked; hooliganism is now virtually non-existent in the grounds and most stadiums are comfortable, safe places. But it is a terrible indictment of the game that it required a series of avoidable disasters before it was forced to take action.

From Slaves to Masters – 1885 to 1998

From the day the Football Association reluctantly caved in and accepted professionalism in the game in 1885, players were not seen as traditional employees. A maximum wage was imposed and a limit placed on signing-on fees. Gradually a transfer market evolved, whereby a club 'sold' a player to another club. The player had little choice. Either he complied with the wishes of the club that held his contract, or he didn't play professional football at all. Once he had signed, he could not choose to move to another employer unless his club agreed. This remarkable set of conditions – a modified form of slavery known as 'retain and transfer' – persisted until 1961, when the maximum wage ruling was also abolished. Full freedom of movement, however, was only achieved in 1995.

At the beginning of the century, transfer fees were quick to escalate in value. In 1905, when the

1954 Wolves, the League champions, beat Honved 3–2. The Hungarian club side was largely made up of the national team and this prompted the Wolves manager, Stan Cullis, to boast that Wolves were the unofficial champions of the world

1955 Stan Cullis's boast prompted L'Equipe, the French sports newspaper, to initiate the European Cup. Fifa sanctioned the tournament, but the Football League refused permission for the English champions, Chelsea, to participate

1956 Manchester City won the FA Cup by beating Birmingham City 3–1 despite the fact that their goalkeeper, Bert Trautman, played with a broken neck after a collision. Trautman only discovered his injury three days after the game

average fee was around £400 and players were not allowed to earn more than £208 a year, Middlesbrough, desperate to avoid relegation, lashed out an astronomical £1,000 to purchase Alf Common from Sunderland. The nation was scandalised that such a sum of money should change hands for a mere football player. Middlesbrough were unabashed, and Common's goals helped them to avoid relegation. The FA's response to the Common transfer was to set a ceiling of £350. Three months later the policy was abandoned, when it was accepted that it was unworkable – clubs could easily circumvent it.

As the game became more and more popular, with ever-increasing attendances, it began to generate serious revenue. The players, however, were not the beneficiaries. A maximum wage of £4 a week had been set in 1900 and was still the maximum in 1907, when 500 footballers met in the Imperial Hotel in Manchester to form the Players' Union. Their grievances were two-fold: the maximum wage and freedom of contract. Ironically, the more successful clubs wanted to raise the maximum wage, but were continually voted down by the less successful clubs, who claimed they couldn't afford it and therefore would not be able to sign quality players. Although the fledgling union flourished in terms of membership, its attempts at organising industrial action to improve the players' lot failed to materialise, so, in 1912, the union turned to the courts. This proved to be a costly mistake.

On the face of it, the Players' Union had found an extremely good case to test the clubs' draconian hold over their players. Aston Villa had fallen out with one of their players, Kingaby, and

1956 Accrington Stanley fielded a team entirely composed of Scots

1956 Real Madrid won the first European Cup final by beating Rheims 4–3 in Paris. Alfredo di Stefano scored all of Real's goals and Real went on to win the next four finals

1956 Matt Busby defied the Football League and entered League champions Manchester United in the second European Cup competition. They reached the semi-final, losing to Real Madrid

1957 Celtic thrashed Rangers 7–1 in the Scottish League Cup final, the biggest score in any British final

1958 The aeroplane carrying the Manchester United team back from a European fixture crashed at Munich airport with twenty-three passengers dying, including eight of the 'Busby Babes'. A makeshift United made it to the FA Cup final but lost 2–0 to Bolton

George Eastham, whose transfer from Newcastle to Arsenal led to the abolition of the maximum wage

had punished him by setting his transfer fee artificially high. This had kept Kingaby out of the game for two years. Unfortunately, the lawyers acting for the union based their case on Aston Villa's motives, claiming that they were malicious. They did not challenge the basis of the actual system of retain and transfer. The judge ruled in favour of the club. The Union had accidentally allowed the system to be enshrined in law.

The maximum wage only went up by niggardly amounts and by 1946 was £8 a week. A threatened strike by the union was averted when it was raised to £9. By 1961, the maximum wage was £20 during the season and £17 in the summer, but this was the era of £100,000 transfers, and the disparity was blindingly obvious. The Players' Union, renamed the Professional Footballers' Association, had campaigned continually against the maximum

1958 Brazil, inspired by the seventeen–year-old Pele, won the World Cup in Sweden by beating the host nation 5–2 in the final

1959 The two regional Third Divisions became a Third and Fourth Division

1959 Billy Wright, the England captain, became the first man in the world to win 100 international caps

1959 Joe Baker of Hibs became the first player at a Scottish club to play for England

wage and the retain and transfer system, to no avail. Matters came to a head when George Eastham, a Newcastle player who wanted to be transferred to Arsenal, announced he was going to take his case to court, claiming Newcastle's refusal to grant him a transfer was a restraint of trade. Militancy was in the air and the PFA finally extracted the abolition of the maximum wage from the Football League. However, the League would not relent over the retain and transfer system. The chairman of the PFA, Jimmy Hill, called it 'a slave contract' and the PFA decided to call a strike. Incredibly, the League retaliated by ordering clubs to play their fixtures the day before the strike was due to begin. The public were outraged at the League's crassness and, with the tide of opinion going against them, the League were finally forced to back down and change the rules that had effectively tied a player to a club for life. Clubs now had to grant a player a transfer if he requested one. But this was not 'real' freedom of contract.

The issue would not go away and, just before the 1977–8 season started, more than 100 players in the Midlands voted to strike over the issue. Support for the PFA spread throughout the country, the League called an extraordinary general meeting and a compromise was hammered out. Players would be free to choose between clubs as long as the two clubs could agree on the fee. If they couldn't, then the dispute would be referred to an independent tribunal. The PFA were not happy with the compromise. 'The position remains unchanged', their secretary Cliff Lloyd said. 'Players are completely in the hands of the club.'

It took an obscure Belgian footballer, Jean-Marc Bosman, finally to break the shackles that bound

1960 Burnley became League champions by winning their final game of the season. It was the first time that they had headed the table all season. Burnley deprived Wolves, the runners-up by a point and the FA Cup-winners, of the first Double by an English club in the century

1960 Real Madrid beat Eintracht Frankfurt 7–3 at Hampden Park to win their fifth, successive European Cup. The match is regarded as one of the greatest ever played

1960 A players' strike was averted when the Football League abolished the maximum wage and conceded that players were not tied to their clubs for life

players to clubs. Bosman had been transferred to RFC Liège in 1988 on a two-year contract. When that expired, Liège offered him a new contract but with a drop in salary of 60 per cent. Bosman refused the contract and said that he wanted to play for Dunkerque. Liège then demanded a transfer fee of more than £250,000 – twice the amount the French club were offering. This deadlock left Bosman unable to earn his living as a footballer. Bosman found himself a lawyer and began a legal process that ultimately was resolved in the European Court of Justice in 1995. The court ruled that Liège's actions had been a restraint of trade. It was a landmark decision. The court also ruled that the current transfer system was in breach of the European law affecting free movement of workers within the European Union and that restrictions on the number of European Union nationals permitted in Uefa competitions were also unlawful.

The PFA were horrified by the final ruling, believing that a flood of overseas players into the domestic game would deny their own members the opportunity to work. And to some extent, this has happened. But, for a non-EU foreign player to get a work permit in Britain, they have to satisfy certain guidelines as to their proven ability and play a specified number of first-team games for their club for it to be renewed.

In a further ruling, the court decided that freedom of movement only applied to out-of-contract European Union nationals moving between member states. In other words, the transfer system in Britain between British clubs would be much the same. However, when a player came to the end of his contract, unless he was offered a new one

1961 Spurs became the first team to win the Double in the twentieth century when they beat Leicester City 2–0 in the Cup final

1962 Accrington Stanley, one of the original founders of the Football League, were wound up and had to resign from the League

1962 Brazil retained the World Cup in Chile when they beat Czechoslovakia 3–1 in the final

1963 Alf Ramsey was appointed England manager. Immediately announced: 'England will win the World Cup.' England were to host the tournament in 1966

1963 Tottenham became the first British club to win a European trophy when they beat Atletico Madrid 5–1 in the final of the European Cup Winners Cup

on the same, or better terms, he would be free to leave without any transfer fee. Also, the ruling would not affect any deals between European Union clubs and non-European Union clubs.

The long-term effect will be that much of the money that previously went on transfer fees will now go into the players' pockets in high wages and large signing-on fees. Players will also enjoy greater job security, as clubs will sign them to longer and longer contracts to prevent losing them to other clubs without any compensation. And it is by no means certain that domestic transfers are exempt from the Bosman ruling. This has yet to be tested in court by a British 'Bosman'. It took a long time, and one very stubborn Belgian, but the dog was finally wagging the tail.

The Match that Began the Boom – a Personal View from an England Supporter

If you wished to choose a year that marked the birth of the new era of English football, a good case could be made for selecting 1990. And an exact day? Without hesitation I would plump for 1 July, the night that England played Cameroon, the Indomitable Lions, in the San Paolo stadium in Naples in the quarter-finals of Italia 90.

The bare facts of the match are in the reference books. With eight minutes to go England were 2–1 down. A Gary Lineker penalty forced extra time and a second Lineker penalty ensured that England played West Germany in the semi-finals. But the facts do no justice to the tense drama of that particular game, nor to the full significance of the result. Yes, England secured a berth in the World Cup semi-finals – but they unwittingly achieved a lot more than that.

1963 Luxembourg knocked Holland out of the European championships 3–2 on aggregate to reach the quarter-finals Both legs were played in Holland

1964 Ten players were banned from the game after revelations that they had been involved in fixing matches to stage betting coups. Among them were two English internationals, Peter Swan and Tony Kay. All ten were eventually sent to jail

1965 Leeds missed out on the championship to Manchester United by 0.686 of a goal and lost the Cup final in extra time 2–1 to Liverpool

1965 Stanley Matthews, at fifty years and five days of age, became the oldest man to play a First Division match. He retired at the end of the season and was knighted

With the clock running down, every England supporter's nightmare was being re-lived in every home in the country. Another failure on the world's biggest stage. And to whom? To a bloody Third World country, for God's sake. With two unflappable strikes, Lineker personally rescued a nation from suicidal despair. Faith and credibility in the English national team, the flagship of the sport, were instantly restored. The semi-final three days later produced the biggest British television audience in history as 26 million people abandoned the pubs, the restaurants and the streets in seething expectation of yet another pulsating victory. (By contrast only 14 million people voted Conservative in the 1992 General Election.)

The boom in English football was born. When the England team returned home from Italy they were mobbed by tens of thousands of fans at Luton airport, many of them young women. From 1990, England internationals at Wembley now had a new batch of fans: 'girlies', as many of them ironically described themselves. And this translated into domestic fixtures as well, with more women attending matches than ever before. It was no accident that the attendance for the first day of the 1990–1 season was the highest for nine years. Total attendances for League matches that season were also up on the previous season, and have been steadily climbing ever since, breaking the 20 million barrier in 1991–2.

Television was not slow to recognise the commercial value of this upswing in football's fortunes and, by May of 1992, after a fierce auction, the fledgling Premier League had negotiated a deal with the BBC and BSkyB worth £304 million over five years. ITV, soundly beaten

1965 West Ham became the second British side to win a European trophy when they beat Munich 1860 2–0 in the European Cup Winners Cup final

1965 Northampton were promoted to the First Division for the first time having worked their way up from the Fourth Division in five seasons. By 1969 they were back in the Fourth Division

1965 Substitutes were introduced into the game

1965 Frank Saul was the first Spurs player to be sent off since 1928

1966 The FA lost the World Cup trophy when a thief broke into the Central Hall, Westminster. It was found a week later by a dog, Pickles. The mongrel attended the celebration banquet after the tournament was over

1966 Real Madrid, and their veteran winger Francisco Gento, won their sixth European Cup when they beat Partizan Belgrade 2–1 in the final

by their rivals to the plum prize, snapped up the Football League matches and the League Cup as their consolation prize. Even Channel 4 were swept up in the soccer craze and proved the demand was insatiable by successfully, and profitably, screening live Italian football league matches on Sunday lunchtimes. Some weeks it is possible to watch live football on television five days of the week, and highlights and previews on the others.

Such blanket television coverage spawned valuable spin-offs. Sponsors began queuing up to take advantage of all this air time. Clubs churned out a plethora of replica team strips and the kids, or rather their parents, bought them in droves. Top flight clubs hiked their ticket prices outrageously, but demand frequently outstrips supply. Manchester United are a multi-million pound business, with the bulk of their income coming from off-the-field activities rather than through the turnstiles. United even have their own magazine, with a circulation in excess of 100,000.

Marketing techniques have become more and more sophisticated. When Tottenham's sponsorship contract with Holsten expired in 1995, Alan Sugar, the club's chairman, negotiated a £4 million deal with Hewlett Packard, the computer firm. But this was only one aspect of the deal. By dropping a lager firm, Tottenham were able to sell their replica kit to the under-18s. Sugar estimated that this was worth several more million. Modern football clubs no longer underestimate the fiscal power of merchandising and sponsorship. For example, independent consumer research proved that Arsenal supporters were more likely to buy JVC electronic equipment than any other brand,

1966 England, the hosts, won the World Cup when they beat West Germany 4–2 after extra time

1967 Second Division Berwick Rangers knocked Rangers out of the Scottish Cup 1–0 in the first round

1967 Scotland beat England, the world champions, 3–2 at Wembley

1967 Celtic became the first British side to win the European Cup when they beat Inter Milan 2–1 in the final

1968 Leeds ended their trophy famine by beating Arsenal 1–0 in the League Cup final and beating Ferencvaros 1–0 on aggregate in the two-legged European Fairs Cup final. In the previous four years, Leeds had twice been championship runners-up, losing Cup finalists and losing Fairs Cup finalists

simply because they were Arsenal's sponsors and their name was on the Arsenal shirt, which, as loyal fans, they frequently wore.

By the mid-1990s the game in England was awash with money. Transfer fees went through the roof. In 1979 the nation was aghast when Brian Clough paid £1 million for Trevor Francis. Yet when Alex Ferguson handed over £7 million for Andy Cole in 1995 many commentators sagely conceded that it was probably a shrewd deal. A year later, Kevin Keegan paid £15 million for Alan Shearer, a world record at the time. Nobody batted an eyelid. Players' salaries also rocketed, with a number earning in excess of £20,000 a week – before bonuses and incentives. Agents, some of them extremely dubious characters, mushroomed. The downside of all of this cash sloshing around was undoubtedly the 'sleaze' phenomenon that has rocked the game in the 1990s, with relentless allegations of 'bungs'. It was alleged in court that the Nottingham Forest manager, Brian Clough, had accepted a 'bung' to facilitate the transfer of Teddy Sheringham from Forest to Spurs. The downfall of George Graham at Arsenal was the direct result of such an allegation.

So did all this really happen because of the result of one World Cup match on a sticky July night in Naples in 1990? Certainly. Consider what would have happened if England had been unceremoniously bundled out of the competition by Cameroon. England would have slunk home with their tails between their legs. The press would have had a field day with the hapless Bobby Robson and his inept players. 'Fed to the Lions', 'Mauled by Lions' would have been some of the kinder headlines. England would have been

---

1968 The Welsh Cup-holders, Cardiff, reached the semi-finals of the European Cup Winners Cup only to lose 4–3 on aggregate to Hamburg

1968 Alan Mullery became the first England player to be sent off when he was dismissed in the European Championship semi-final against Yugoslavia

1968 Manchester United became the first English side to win the European Cup when they beat Benfica 4–1 after extra time at Wembley

1969 Third Division Swindon beat Arsenal 3–1 after extra time to win the League Cup. They also won promotion

1969 Honduras and El Salvador broke off diplomatic relations after El Salvador had acrimoniously triumphed in a series of World Cup qualifying matches. Then, El Salvador invaded Honduras and bombed military targets and their airport. In the ensuing war over 2,000 people were killed

denied the chance to cover themselves in glory by only losing to the eventual world champions in a nail-biting penalty shoot-out. Gazza would not have been immortalised by his tears. Nor would he have been hailed as the young player of the tournament and Gazza-mania would not have got off the ground. It is also likely that Lazio would not have subsequently paid Tottenham £8.5 million for his services.

England's success in 1990 – officially crowned as one of the four best sides in the world – produced a cultural sea-change. Perhaps it started when, later that week, a female columnist in the quality press wrote that, until that night, football had held no interest for her. But as the drama unfolded against Cameroon, she said, she had nearly died from the nerve-jangling excitement. Overnight it became fashionable to talk about football at dinner parties, in restaurants and to write about it in places other than the sports pages.

In the same year, a cover story on Patsy Kensit in the *Sunday Times* Magazine began with several hundred words on her obsession with football, 'outing' her as a closet Spurs fan when she was publicly supposed to be a [Glasgow] Rangers fan. Other celebrities came out of the closet voluntarily. The screen writers Anthony Minghella and Alan Plater wrote lyrical pieces in sports pages about their passionate love affairs with their football clubs, Portsmouth and Hull respectively. John Major and David Mellor tried to demonstrate their common touch by professing their loyalty to Chelsea FC. Football also invaded the West End of London with the highly successful play *An Evening with Gary Lineker* about football supporters on holiday experiencing the agony of the 1990 semi-final

1970 The England captain, Bobby Moore, was arrested in Bogota, Colombia, on suspicion of stealing a bracelet just before the World Cup in Mexico. The charges were dropped when the witness disappeared

1970 Brazil won the World Cup in Mexico by beating Italy 4–1 in the final

1970 The Italian striker, Luigi Riva, broke the arm of a spectator with a wild shot. A few days later Riva broke his leg while playing for Italy

1971 Arsenal became the second club in the twentieth century to win the Double when they beat Liverpool 2–1 after extra time in the Cup final. Ironically, Arsenal had snatched the League title five days earlier by beating their bitter rivals Spurs at White Hart Lane. A decade earlier, Spurs had become the first team to do the Double in modern times

against West Germany. It was a novel experience for the theatre staff who were nonplussed by the content of the play and the demand for seats. Everybody reserving a ticket was dutifully told: 'You do realise that Gary Lineker is not actually going to be on stage.' (The play was later filmed for television.) A memorable line was the description of Lineker as 'the Queen Mother of football', a sobriquet neatly exploited by Walker's crisps in a television advertising campaign where Lineker steals crisps from a young boy and a cheque from a nun with the punch-line: 'No more Mr Nice Guy.' The impact of the advert can be gauged from the 23 complaints received by the Independent Television Complaints board and the number of letters to newspapers from those who enjoyed the joke and those who didn't.

The cultural assimilation of football was everywhere:

Gazza 'immortalised by his tears'

Eric Cantona even modelled clothes on a Parisian catwalk. One of the most extraordinary examples of football's renaissance was the runaway success of Nick Hornby's book *Fever Pitch*. It was the most unlikely of best-sellers. An anguished, autobiographical account of how a schoolboy became a diehard Arsenal supporter in order to survive a broken home. Arsenal? The most unloved club in the country? Adolescent angst? It was the *Catcher in the Rye* of football and a runaway best-seller. Inevitably, it was the Sports Book of the Year in 1992 and turned Hornby into a postmodern football celebrity.

But back to the match that shook up the world of English football. Just what was so special about that particular game?

First, the Cameroon match has to be taken in conjunction with the West Germany match. Obviously the second game had the greater historical significance, but if England had not won the first, the second match would not have taken place. What was at stake was a tantalising semi-final against the ancient foe, West Germany. (Despite what the Scots believe, English fans look across the North Sea for their bitter rivals, not Hadrian's Wall.)

Also, we were sick of living off the World Cup glories of the dim and distant past of 1966 (when we won the whole thing) and 1970 (when we were almost the measure of the best-ever Brazilian side and threw away a 2–0 lead against West Germany in the quarter-finals). After that we failed to qualify for the finals of 1974 and 1978; were out-thought in 1982 and cheated by Diego Maradona in 1986. England fans were hungry for some recent success.

1971 Fourth Division Colchester, with six players over the age of thirty, knocked Leeds out of the FA Cup 3–2

1971 A late equaliser in the Old Firm game at Ibrox caused departing fans to try to return to the game. In the confusion, crush barriers collapsed and in the ensuing panic, 66 people were killed and over 200 injured

1971 A referee's decision to allow an offside goal at Elland Road sparked a riot. Incensed Leeds fans invaded the pitch and tried to manhandle the referee. The 'goal' cost Leeds the game and, ultimately, the championship

1972 Non-League Hereford knocked First Division Newcastle out of the FA Cup 2–1 after extra time in a third round replay. At the end of the season Hereford were elected as members of the Football League

The fans were also fully aware that England had scraped into the quarter-finals in 1990. Only Paul Gascoigne's indefatigable brilliance – he ran fifty yards to win a free-kick in the last twinkling of extra time and then coolly floated the ball over the defence to David Platt – prevented a penalty shoot-out with Belgium. Moreover, the England team were ready-made for Cameroon: it traditionally plays like petrified postmen against underdogs. And Cameroon were underdogs with a pedigree: a ball-playing, attacking side who had humiliated Argentina 1–0 in the opening match of Italia 90. Fans and players feared the worst. 'Anything can happen in Cup football', the players kept saying before the game. 'Look what Palace did to Liverpool in the FA Cup semi-final.' (Palace won 4–3, having lost 9–0 in the League.) That was the backdrop.

The first twenty minutes were murder as it was obvious Cameroon were up for it. We could have given away a penalty, Cameroon fluffed a couple of chances and then ... bang. In the twenty-fifth minute Platt rose to meet Pearce's cross with a point blank, unstoppable header. And yet ... although we held out at 1–0 to half-time, Cameroon were still stringing their act together. Just after the hour, the leaky roof that was England's defence caved in. Twice. First, Gazza brought down Roger Milla, Cameroon's thirty-eight-year-old shaven-haired talisman, and Kunde scored from the spot. Then, three minutes later, Milla chipped a beautiful ball to Ekeke (who had just come on as a substitute) and Cameroon were in the driving seat at 2–1 with twenty-six minutes to go.

This was the stomach-curdling bit, where minutes fly past like seconds and you wonder why you have volunteered to undergo this ordeal. The lady columnist wasn't alone. Millions in England were

1972 Derby won the championship while they were on a beach in Majorca as all their rivals faltered in their final matches

1972 One man died, 150 were injured, and hundreds arrested when celebrating Rangers fans invaded the pitch after their team won the European Cup Winners Cup and were confronted by Spanish riot police

1973 Liverpool became the first English team to win the League title and a European trophy in the same season when they captured the Uefa Cup by beating Borussia Moenchengladbach 3–2 on aggregate

1973 Celtic became the first club to win the Scottish title eight years in succession. A year later they won their ninth to equal the world record for successive championships

experiencing the same pain and the same passion. As I paced my floor in front of the television set, my heart pounding and my skin clammy with a thin film of sweat, I suddenly remembered I had never made a will. I quickly told my wife. Then, with eight minutes left, England were awarded a penalty and we were level. The pain eased, but it was too early to taste any pleasure. Thoughts of writing a will were banished, as we waited for extra time to arrive.

A quick check of the reference books. Yes, it was only the third penalty that England had been awarded in ninety-one games under Bobby Robson's stewardship. It had been clear-cut and even the Mexican referee had to give it. Kunde, who had scored their penalty, brought Lineker down just as he was about to score. With the whole of England half not wanting to watch, Lineker

Gary Lineker scores England's winner from the penalty spot in extra time

coolly slotted it home as easily as Tiger Woods sinks a short putt. So, despite being out-played for much of the game, we were level. Mark Wright, who had set up Lineker's foray into the area, clashed with Milla and received a bloody head wound. We were effectively down to ten men, but the tide had turned. We were now on the wave, not Cameroon.

So it proved in extra time. Oh they fought, those Lions, and Peter Shilton had to be at his best to keep them at bay. Once again Gazza rose to the occasion. With 105 minutes gone, he burst through the Cameroon team and presented Lineker with a pass of diamond precision, shredding their defence and leaving N'Kono, their goalkeeper, in a desperate situation. He sent Lineker crashing and the England striker duly dispatched the fourth penalty in Robson's reign. Ecstasy. The game wasn't officially over by any means: Cameroon strove valiantly for the equaliser, England to consolidate their lead. But back home we knew it was over. The script had had its fill of twists and turns, and the curtain eventually fell on a famous victory.

One of the problems with such nights is that there are too many words and clichés to describe the gamut of emotions experienced by both the players and spectators, and they usually all end up in print or on television. It can be likened to war: 'Cameroon met their Waterloo'; or erotic love: 'England's orgasmic climax'; or death: 'Lions' throats slit by the bulldogs'. In a sense all of these are true. The intensity of the contest, the importance placed on it by its aficionados, and the beauty and grace of the physical confrontation raises those involved to extraordinary levels. It even touched the soul of a highly-paid lady columnist on a posh paper.

1973 Ajax won the European Cup for the third year in succession when they beat Juventus 1–0

1974 Sir Alf Ramsey was sacked six months after England failed to qualify for the World Cup finals. He was replaced by Don Revie, the Leeds manager

1974 Three different players took the same penalty for Notts County against Portsmouth and they all failed to score

1974 The Soviet Union withdrew from the World Cup because they refused to play a qualifying match against Chile, where a military coup had ousted the Marxist president, Salvador Allende, and the stadium had been used to imprison and torture republican loyalists

1974 West Germany, the hosts, won the World Cup when they beat Holland 2–1. Holland's goal was scored from a penalty in the first few seconds without a German having touched the ball

Free-Kicks

A direct free-kick permits the player taking the kick to score without the ball having to touch anybody else. In the case of an indirect free-kick, however, the ball must be touched by another player, of either side, before a goal can be legally scored. If the referee awards an indirect free-kick, he will signal this by raising an arm above his head. He will keep it in that position until the ball has been played or touched by another player or goes out of play. To indicate a direct free-kick, the referee blows his whistle and points to the spot from where the kick should be taken.

A direct free-kick is awarded when a player is:

• kicking, or attempting to kick, an opponent
• tripping an opponent
• jumping at an opponent
• charging an opponent in a violent or dangerous manner
• tackling an opponent before contacting the ball
• striking, or attempting to strike, an opponent
• holding an opponent
• pushing an opponent
• deliberately handling the ball. This does not apply to the goalkeeper, providing he is within the penalty area
• spitting at a player, an official or other persons.

The kick is taken from the spot where the incident occurred. If any of these offences are committed inside the penalty area by a defending player, then a penalty is awarded and taken from the penalty spot. When a free-kick is being taken, all of the opposing players must be at least ten yards from the ball, unless they are standing on their own goal-line between the goal posts. At a penalty-kick, all players must stand behind the penalty spot at a distance of ten yards, indicated by the D.

An indirect free-kick is awarded when a player is:

• playing in a dangerous manner, for example, trying to kick the ball out of the goalkeeper's hands
• charging an opponent when the ball is not within playing distance
• obstructing an opponent
• time-wasting, including goalkeepers holding on to the ball for more than five/six seconds
• offside
• taking a penalty or a corner-kick and plays the ball a second time before it has touched another player
• a goalkeeper takes more than four steps while holding the ball
• a goalkeeper uses his hands to take possession of a ball passed to him by a teammate, excluding headed and chested balls but including throw-ins

Offside

• A player is in an offside position if he is nearer to his opponents' goal-line than at least two of his opponents (one of which is usually the goalkeeper) when the ball has been played forward by a teammate.
• A player is not offside:
a) if he is in his own half of the field
b) if he is not involved in active play and not gaining an advantage by being offside
c) if he receives the ball direct from a goal-kick, corner-kick or throw-in
• Offside is judged from the moment the ball is played, not when a player receives the pass. In

other words, a player does not become offside if he goes forward during the flight of the ball, so long as he starts his run from an onside position when the ball is kicked

Discipline

A caution is signalled by a yellow card and a dismissal by a red one. In both instances the referee will make a note of the player's name. If a player receives two yellow cards in the same match he will be automatically dismissed. In this case, the referee shows a yellow card followed by a red card.

A player will be cautioned if he:

• enters or re-enters the field of play, or deliberately leaves the field of play without the referee's permission
• persistently infringes the Laws of the Game
• shows dissent from any decision by the referee
• is guilty of unsporting behaviour, which has recently encompassed 'diving'
• does not retire to the proper distance at a free-kick or encroaches at a penalty
• dances about or gesticulates in a way designed to distract opponents while a free-kick or throw-in is being taken
• delays the re-start of play
• a goalkeeper lies on the ball longer than necessary

A player will be sent off if he:

• is guilty of violent conduct or serious foul play
• uses offensive, insulting or abusive language, or spits at opponents, officials or other persons
• persists in misconduct after a caution, for example persistent encroachment at a free-kick

• illegally prevents an obvious scoring opportunity (often described as a 'professional foul')
• tackles from behind (this was re-emphasised by Fifa for the 1998 World Cup)

Punishment (British League Competitions)

Players are banned for one to three games after five bookings and a further ban of one to two matches is imposed after eight. Players with eleven bookings have to face an FA disciplinary committee. All bookings are treated equally, no matter what the offence. Players who are sent off are banned for between one and three games depending on the severity of the offence that led to the dismissal. Players sent off for a second caution in a match are treated differently from those who are automatically dismissed, and will only usually be suspended for one match. As an incentive to promote fair play, the FA remove one booking from a player's record if he goes five full games without either a booking or a sending-off.

Substitutes

Teams in the English and Scottish Premier Leagues are allowed to make three substitutions from a named panel of five which can include a goalkeeper. The number of players on the panel varies in other competitions. The referee must be informed of the proposed substitution before it is made. The player being substituted must leave the field before the substitute can come on, and then only when the referee has signalled that he can do so. The substituted player can take no further part in the match. The substitute can only come on when there is a stoppage in play, and then only from the halfway line.

'It only takes a second to score a goal.'
Brian Clough

Of all the astute observations on football and tactics made by one of football's most colourful managers, that particular assertion is perhaps the most acute. Over the decades, many matches seemingly lost have been transformed by the scoring of a goal and hopeless causes turned into glorious come-from-behind victories. Such instant reverses of fortune are the bane of the scientific manager with his 'Christmas tree' formation and his overlapping wing-backs. Theory goes out the window with a flash of inspiration, a deflection, a casual back-pass, or whatever. And sometimes the theoretician will claim that an 'accidental' goal was the result of some fiendish scheming.

Martin O'Neill loves to tell the story of how Nottingham Forest retained the European Cup against Hamburg in 1980 when he was playing for Clough and Peter Taylor. Forest were forced to play with a depleted side and their goalkeeper, Peter Shilton, limped through the game with a pain-killing injection because of a pulled calf muscle. Hamburg were led by the mercurial Kevin Keegan and Clough and Taylor were understandably wary in their approach to the final. So when, according to O'Neill, the Forest midfield launched a counter-attack in the twentieth minute and worked the ball to winger John Robertson, Clough and Taylor leapt off the bench and frantically waved to their players telling them to get back in their own half. The arm-waving turned to hugs when Robertson unleashed a thunderous shot from outside the area that went in off the post. Seventy minutes of dour defending later and Clough was able to claim:

1974 Pele retired. He played the first twenty minutes of a match for Santos and then left the pitch in tears

1975 Leeds were banned from European competition for four years after their fans rioted in Paris during their 2–0 defeat by Bayern Munich in Paris in the European Cup final

1976 Bayern Munich won the European Cup for the third year in a row by beating St Etienne 1–0

1976 An FA committee attempted to ban 'kissing and cuddling' after a goal was scored. The idea was thrown out because it was impracticable

1977 Hearts, despite having reached the semi-finals of the Scottish Cup and League Cup, were relegated for the first time in 103 years

'The odds were stacked against us but it was the best 90 minutes we ever had. It was absolutely marvellous.'

It's players who win or lose games, not systems. But systems make a difference. When Hungary humiliated England twice in 1953 and 1954 – beating them 6–3 at Wembley and 7–1 in Budapest – for sure they were embarrassed by the fabulous skills of Ferenc Puskas, Sandor Kocsis, Nandor Hidegkuti and the rest of the Magnificent Magyars. But they were also tactically bamboozled by Hungary's deployment of Hidegkuti as a deep-lying centre-forward behind their own strikeforce, and the wily Magyars constantly drew England's stopper centre-half out of position. It is highly unlikely that England could have withstood that marvellous team; however a little tactical acumen might have prevented their being routed twice.

John Robertson (dark shirt, right) lashes home Nottingham Forest's winning goal against Hamburg in the 1980 European Cup final

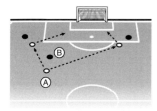

Deep-lying centre-forward (A) pulls the opposing centre-half (B) out of position leaving space for his teammates to attack the goal

1977 Scotland's fifth victory on English soil since 1938, when they won 2–1 at Wembley, caused their fans to break both goals, cut out swathes of the turf and get arrested

1977 Liverpool became the second English club to win the European Cup when they beat Borussia Moenchengladbach 3–1 in Rome in the final

1977 Don Revie, the England manager, knowing full well that England couldn't qualify for the World Cup final, deserted the job for a lucrative post in the United Arab Emirates. Ron Greenwood, the West Ham manager, replaced him

For some in English football, those two games were a watershed. Not that they immediately ushered in a new era of modern, strategic methods of play, but they certainly caused some people to put on their thinking caps. Don Revie was one. The Manchester City player studied the Hungarians' methods and turned himself into a deep-lying centre-forward, Magyar style. In the 1956 FA Cup final against the favourites, Birmingham City, Revie deployed the tactic with consummate skill and the Manchester club waltzed off with the Cup.

For others, the Continental style of possession football was anathema and they had a boffin to prove it. Behind the scenes, a retired wing commander, Charles Reep, had been meticulously analysing the amount of possession a team had in a match and the goal yield. His statistical conclusion was that the fewer the number of passes, the more likely it was that a goal would be scored. Goals were rarely scored if they involved more than three touches. Therefore, to score more goals – and thus win more games – teams should mount as many simple, unfussy attacks as possible. This hypothesis came to be known as 'long-ball theory', where the ball is launched into the opposing team's last quarter of the pitch – frequently by-passing the midfield – as often as possible – and complex passing plays eschewed. Reep also noticed that a number of goals come from 'accidental happenings', mistakes made by defenders, the odd bounce of the ball, deflections and the like. By keeping the ball in the target area as much as possible, the law of averages would suggest that fortune will eventually favour the attacking side. Reep may have been an eccentric, but he had his devotees. Stan Cullis, the manager of Wolverhampton Wanderers in the 1950s, was one of them.

Playing long-ball, Wolves won the championship three times in that decade and were runners-up twice. More significantly, perhaps, was a series of friendly matches Wolves played against top overseas clubs in 1954–5. Not only did the English champions emerge unbeaten, but one of their prized scalps was Honved, the Hungarian club side that included Ferenc Puskas and contained many of the national team that so easily overran England. Thus began a polarised debate between the advocates of kick and run and those who advanced a more composed, thoughtful style of play. As an example of the latter, the 1951 Tottenham side, managed by Arthur Rowe, won the championship playing 'push and run' – a term he hated because it did not adequately describe the intricate, short, triangular passing movements on which it was based. The concept was developed by Rowe with his senior players in a dining car on a train, when the manager used a number of salt and pepper cruets to demonstrate to his players just why they were playing so well. The demonstration became a strategy. Rowe's catchphrase for this playing style was: 'Make it simple, make it accurate, make it quick.' And in 1961, that team's successors, now managed by Billy Nicholson, became the first club to win the Double of League championship and FA Cup in the same season this century. That Spurs side's tactics were a development of Rowe's. And the Liverpool teams that virtually swept all before them in the late 1970s and the 1980s took the basic philosophy and refined it even further.

But, before we get carried away with the idea that a football match is a chess game masterminded by a

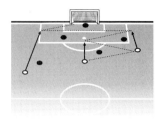

The intricate passing movements of Tottenham's 'push and run' strategy

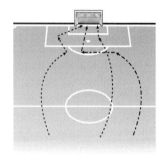

The 'long ball' game, effective with the right players but not pretty to watch

1978 The High Court upheld the FA's ban on twelve-year-old schoolgirl playing for a boys' team

1978 Liverpool became the first English club to retain the European Cup when they beat Bruges 1–0 at Wembley in the final

1978 Argentina, the hosts, won the World Cup when they beat Holland 3–1 after extra time

cunning strategist and the players merely pawns in his grand plan, it is worth pointing out that much of the 'coaching' before the 1960s and 1970s in the British game was laughable. Frequently, the manager's advice to his team just before they took the field was: 'Go out and enjoy yourself.' So-called training often did not involve the use of a ball at all. 'If they don't see it until Saturday, they'll be hungry for it', was the profound thinking behind this piece of homespun football wisdom. However, for every dozen buffoons purporting to act as 'managers' there would be at least one tactician at the helm – a Clough, a Cullis, a Rowe or a Nicholson. The problem for British football was that the buffoons could, and did, stem the tide of innovation. An example of how entrenched this backwardness was comes from a football journalist's remark at the end of the 1960 European Cup final at Hampden. Real Madrid and Eintracht Frankfurt had just put on the most dazzling display of football ever seen in the British Isles and 127,000 spectators were spellbound. So much so, that they wouldn't leave the stadium, they just wanted to gawp at the empty pitch. The journalist turned to a colleague and shocked him by dismissing Real's awesome 7–3 victory with the words: 'It was exciting, but it'll never catch on.'

This split over modernity, styles of play and the need for tactics, became a fissure. Continental sides refined and developed their sophisticated mode of playing, while English football tended to pursue more direct play. Unheralded, Reep continued to act as a private consultant to a number of clubs, studying over 3,000 matches, and it was his thinking that was behind Watford's meteoric rise under Graham Taylor's managership from the Fourth Division to the FA Cup final and runners-

1978 Nottingham Forest's Viv Anderson became the first black player to play for England

1979 Nottingham Forest broke the British transfer record by paying Birmingham City £1 million for Trevor Francis

1979 A Cup-tie between Inverness Thistle and Falkirk was postponed a record twenty-nine times. The game was eventually played forty-seven days after it was originally scheduled

1980 The Football League agreed to award three points for a win

1981 Crystal Palace had five different managers in thirteen months

1982 Football's first streaker, Variania Scotney, was a seventeen-year-old waitress who ran across the Highbury pitch topless as Arsenal were losing 3–1 to Spurs

up spot in the championship in the late 1970s and early 1980s. Charles Hughes, a director of coaching at the Football Association, adopted similar ideas to Reep's and incorporated them into the official FA coaching manual. Long-ball theory had been given its imprimatur.

It is a debate that still rages today, although Charles Hughes is now retired and, under Glenn Hoddle as England manager, the national side have cultivated a more Continental approach. However, the tendency to hoof hopeful balls into the opposing penalty area – a sort of biff-and-bang attitude – is never far from the heart of English football.

It was ever thus.

The Early Days

If you could watch an English football match from the 1880s you might be forgiven for thinking you had stumbled across a school playground, as swarms of youths chased after the ball in a kind of mass dribbling. Once a forward got the ball, he would attempt to dribble past as many defenders as possible and score. Nobody passed the ball, or crossed it, or even headed it. When a player got near the goal, he would walk it in. Shooting was unheard of. However, by the turn of the century, the game resembled something more akin to what it is today.

The people generally responsible for this were the Scots, where the game was dominated by the working class, as opposed to the south of England, where it was principally the preserve of former public schoolboys. Lured by the prospects of under-the-counter payments and sinecure

1982 Italy won the World Cup in Spain by beating West Germany 3–1 in the final. Italy had qualified from the first-round group without winning a match. The final four matches that gave them their third World Cup were the only matches they won in the whole of the year

1983 Bob Paisley, who had been Liverpool's manager for nine years, called it a day having secured thirteen major trophies during his term of office

1983 Aberdeen won the European Cup Winners Cup, the third Scottish club to win a European trophy. They also won the Scottish Cup

1983 Tottenham became the first club to be floated on the Stock Exchange and their 3.8 million shares were over-subscribed by more than four times

employment in Lancashire, droves of Scots came over the Border to play for the burgeoning clubs in that county. Most clubs were not content to have one Scottish maestro, some would have as many as six or seven. Apart from the fact that this influx eventually caused the game to embrace professionalism, the Scots' enduring legacy to the game was to introduce the pass. Perhaps the Scots, with their noted acuity, had realised what Oscar Arce, a notable Argentinian coach, was wont to point out to his players nearly one hundred years later: 'The ball, it never gets tired. Pass it.'

Formations were rudimentary, but, early in this century, teams would generally line up with a goalkeeper; four at the back (a right and left half and a right and left back); a centre-half in front of the back four, and five forwards. This structure changed fundamentally in 1925, when the offside law was changed. Previously, there had to be three men (one of whom was usually the goalkeeper) between the attacker and the goal when the ball was last played, otherwise the player would be offside. However, cunning defenders had reduced the game to a farce by exploiting the rule and forty offside decisions a game were commonplace. So in 1925, the number of players required for an attacker to be onside was reduced from three to two.

The effect was extraordinary and unexpected. On the opening day of the new season, Aston Villa scored ten goals, Newcastle seven and Tottenham and Huddersfield drew 5–5. The rule change had opened the goal floodgates. Arsenal, under their legendary manager, Herbert Chapman, were the first to adapt their system to deal with this new problem and, in doing so, created a template for all modern football systems.

1984 All six British clubs involved in European competitions reached the semi-finals. However only Tottenham (Uefa Cup) and Liverpool went on to win their competitions

1984 Liverpool became the third English club to win three successive championships. They also won the European Cup and the League Cup

1984 France won their first major championship when they beat Spain in the final of the European championships 2–0 in Paris

1984 Stirling Albion scored fifteen goals in the first half against Selkirk in the Scottish Cup, winning 20–0. It was the biggest defeat in British football since 1891

1985 Millwall fans rioted during an FA Cup-tie at Luton. Forty-seven people, including thirty-one policemen were injured.

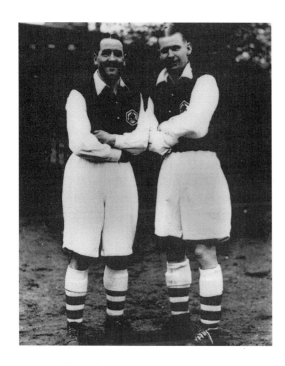

Alex James (left) and Cliff Bastin, two of the forwards from Arsenal's legendary 1930s side. Bastin held the club's scoring record for over fifty years until overtaken by Ian Wright in 1997

The original impetus for this tactical revolution came from Charlie Buchan, the Arsenal captain. Initially, Chapman was unimpressed with Buchan's ideas but, after a 7–0 drubbing at Newcastle, in which the north-east team had used one element of Buchan's scheme, the pair of them thrashed out the new system. Two days after their heavy defeat, the remodelled Arsenal went to West Ham and won 4–0. The two backs had been moved to the wings (previously they had played as a pair in the middle of the back-four). The centre-half no longer had a free, attacking role in the midfield just behind the five-man forward line; instead, he would be an out-and-out defender at the heart of the defence; the two half-backs would play in front of this back three; two forwards, the inside right and left, would

1985 A fire in a wooden stand at Bradford caused the deaths of fifty-six spectators

1985 Non-League Telford battled all the way to the fifth round of the FA Cup before being beaten 3–0 by Everton, the eventual finalists

1985 Thirty-nine Italian fans died at the European Cup final between Juventus and Liverpool in Brussels when a wall collapsed while the Italians were fleeing from charging Liverpool supporters

55

lie behind the three remaining forwards in what became known as the W-formation. The inside forwards would provide the distribution to the two wingers and the centre-forward.

Forged in the goal-glut season of 1925–6, this was essentially a defensive-minded system but had within it the capacity for swift counter-attacks and, as Arsenal were so successful with it in the 1930s, it came to dominate British and much of European football for over three decades. Then the Brazilians unveiled 4–2–4 at the 1958 World Cup in Sweden.

The Modern Era

Italy, under the astute guidance of their coach Vittorio Pozzo, had resolutely refused to bow to the third-back system and had retained the centre-half as an adventurous attacking player, winning the 1934 and 1938 World Cups. But two results shortly after the Second World War dramatically altered their philosophy. In 1947 a combined British side thrashed the Rest of Europe 6–1 at Hampden. A year later, England demolished Italy in Turin 4–0. To the reigning champions of the world, the conclusion was obvious – a more defensive system was needed. However, instead of emulating the British third-back format, they went even further and perfected the most stifling defensive system the game has ever known: *catenaccio*.

The impetus for the system came from Switzerland, where the Austrian coach of their national team, Karl Rappan, had moved the third back even further, to behind the rest of the defence. The Italians embraced the idea with gusto. *Catenaccio* means 'bolt' and now the centre-half would be a 'sweeper', playing behind a four-man

1986 Rangers' newly-appointed manager, Graeme Souness, announced that the club would sign Catholics. Three years later Souness signed the former Celtic player, Mo Johnston, a Catholic

1986 Liverpool became the third English club this century to do the Double

1986 Argentina won their second World Cup when they beat West Germany 3–2 in the final

1987 In their first FA Cup final, Coventry beat Tottenham 3–2 in extra time. Tottenham had won all of their previous seven finals

1989 Ninety-five Liverpool fans were killed and hundreds injured at the FA Cup semi-final at Hillsborough when police allowed too many fans to rush into the Leppings Lane End of the stadium and they were crushed against the perimeter fencing

defence consisting of two full-backs and two centre-backs. In front of them would be two midfielders and three forwards – a 1–4–2–3 formation. Played at its most niggardly, it could be 1–4–3–2, with only two forwards. The sweeper, or *libero* – the free man – was the last line of defence. His job was to bolster the four backs, to cover for any errors, to 'lock the door' if an opposing forward threatened his goal.

Catenaccio dominated Italian football at all levels until the 1970s and was particularly effective in the European Cup in the 1960s. Milan won the trophy twice, 1963 and 1969, and their cross-town rivals, Inter, succeeded in 1964 and 1965. Inter's coach was Helenio Herrera, the demon king of *catenaccio*. His fundamental philosophy was that you began a match with the score 0–0. If it stayed that way, you had secured a draw and, in a League system, a point. If you scored once, and then 'locked the door' for the rest of the match, you had won. Pretty it wasn't. But in the format of European competition, two-legged home and away ties, it was devastatingly effective. You shut up shop in the away leg, and scored at home. Ironically, it was British dash and muscularity that sounded the death-knell for *catenaccio* when Celtic beat Herrera's Inter in the 1967 European Cup final. Brazil put the final nails in the coffin in the 1970 World Cup final in Mexico, when they destroyed Italy 4–1. Not that *catenaccio* would disappear; instead, the Dutch and the West Germans would show that it could be refined into an attacking system.

While the Italians were locked into their sterile philosophy, the World Cup winning teams of Brazil of 1958 and 1962 were tinkering with a more

1989 Arsenal denied the FA Cup-winners, Liverpool, the Double when they won the League championship by beating Liverpool 2–0 at Anfield with the title-clinching goal coming in the last minute

1990 Lord Justice Taylor's report on the Hillsborough disaster recommended that stadiums should be all-seater and that the perimeter fences must come down. The football authorities and the government accepted his recommendations

1990 The English Schools FA changed their constitution to recognise that girls played football

1990 West Germany won their second World Cup when they beat Argentina 1–0 in Italy

1990 The Faroe Islands beat Austria 1–0 in Sweden in the qualifying stages of the European championships. It was their first competitive international fixture

The 17 year-old Pele scores Brazil's third goal in the 1958 World Cup Final game against hosts Sweden. Brazil won 5-2, including a hat-trick from Pele

flamboyant combination of attack and defence. In the 1958 finals – which saw the debut of the seventeen–year-old Pele – Brazil played with a 4–2–4 formation. The flat back-four had two centre-halves flanked by two full-backs. Two midfield players were the links to two genuine wingers and two quasi centre-forwards. Four years later, in the finals in Chile, Brazil had re-shaped again, now it was 4–3–3. This was the formation – Italy excepted – that was the foundation of subsequent modern systems. England modified it, under Alf Ramsey, to win the World Cup in 1966. A Brazilian 4–3–3 would have one of the front three as an out-and-out winger. Ramsey abandoned wingers entirely: when his team beat West Germany in the final at Wembley, the winners were called the 'Wingless Wonders'.

The 1966 World Cup finals were the first to be globally televised by satellite. The 32 matches were watched by 32 billion viewers. Although the systems and specific formations used by the successful national sides in previous tournaments had either been emulated or modified by coaches around the world, the 1966 event had a much bigger impact.

First, everybody could finally see all the matches and second, because Brazil, the darlings of samba football, were dulled by dour, dirty European football as Pele was kicked to pieces. The lack of quality wingers in the Football League prompted Ramsey to build his World Cup-winning side without them and the success of the national side almost obliterated wingers from the English game as club coaches followed the national team's lead.

But in Holland and West Germany, other lessons were being learnt. Franz Beckenbauer with Bayern Munich and Johann Cruyff with Ajax, were, quite independently, revolutionising the game. Both were turning *catenaccio* on its head, and both would be so successful in liberating this sterile system that their national sides would adopt the new philosophy and, in the 1974 World Cup final, the pair would cross swords. The brave new world

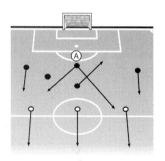

The *libero* (A) moves upfield from a deep defensive position, accompanied by his two backs with a teammate dropping back to cover

The Kaiser, Franz Beckenbauer, West Germany's *libero* supreme

was called, simply, 'Total Football'. And, for a decade, in the 1970s, it swept all before it, both at world and club level.

Beckenbauer's genius was in recognising that it didn't axiomatically follow that the *libero* should be confined to playing behind his defence. If he could move up to bolster the line, why couldn't he advance further? After all, *libero* means free man, so why not truly set him free? Let him go upfield, initiate attacks. Why not? Apart from the goalkeeper, he was the one player on his team that could see the entire pitch. What better place to launch an attack? Thus, the Kaiser, as Beckenbauer was nicknamed, found a method that would combine the adventurous, attacking role of the pre-1925 centre-half with the Italianate last-ditch gatekeeper. Of course, you have to be a particular type of player to assume such an awesome responsibility. You'll need to be wily, able to read the game in a flash and have an astonishing change of pace to shake off opposing players. You will have to possess the abilities of a defender and those of an attacker. Beckenbauer had all this, and an unshakeable belief in his own ability. Could anybody else have done it? Is it systems that win games or players? Whatever the answer to that conundrum, it is certainly true that once Beckenbauer showed the way, others followed.

Cruyff's genius with Ajax and Holland was along similar lines to his German counterpart. Cruyff, however, was a forward. The revolution he inspired was to produce Total footballers: attackers who could, and would, defend. Defenders similarly blessed with attacking skills. Thus, when a defender raced upfield, an attacker would drop back to cover the gap. And if an attacker was forced to defend, a

1992 The English First Division broke away from the Football League and formed the Premiership

1993 Manchester United won their first League championship since 1967

1993 The European champions, Marseilles, were stripped of their titles because of a bribery scandal and relegated to the French Second Division

1993 Almost all of the Zambian national side were killed in a plane crash

1994 Manchester United became the fourth English club this century to win the Double but failed to become the first English side to win the Treble when they lost the League Cup final 3–1 to Aston Villa

1994 Brazil won their fourth World Cup when they beat Italy 3–2 in a penalty shoot-out after a goalless draw in the United States

1994 The Colombian World Cup player, Andres Escobar, was shot dead in Medellin after the tournament where his own-goal had contributed to his team's elimination

Johann Cruyff, the Dutch master who spearheaded Total Football in the early 1970s

defender would move up to ensure that all the attacking options had their full complement. So breathtaking were these teams that some observers thought that the opposition was at its most vulnerable when they had possession of the ball! What if you gave it away? Normally, when an attack breaks down in midfield, you get the ball back quite quickly, but with this renaissance team, anything could happen, such was their versatility. Once again, the question arises: was it the players or the system? For Total Football to work, a coach must have at his disposal intelligent, wonderfully fit, multi-skilled players. Rinus Michels, Cruyff's coach at Ajax and Holland, and the overseer of this revolution once said: 'You need at least seven world-class footballers in the team. One fewer, and it won't work.'

Ajax won the European Cup three years in a row, in 1971, 1972 and 1973. Their 1972 triumph, 2–0 against Inter, was particularly sweet as 'new' *catenaccio* swept aside 'old' *catenaccio*. Then, with Cruyff plying his trade in Barcelona, Beckenbauer and Bayern took over the mantle and lifted the European Cup in the succeeding three years. Total Football had conquered the cream of Europe six years in succession. Total Football had similarly outshone the rest of the world with Holland and West Germany contesting the 1974 World Cup final in Munich, where West Germany were perhaps fortunate to emerge 2–1 winners. Four years later, Holland, without Cruyff, who stubbornly refused to compete, were in the final again, this time against Argentina in Buenos Aires. They lost in extra time. And then, suddenly, Total Football was gone. Beckenbauer and Cruyff eventually became successful managers, Beckenbauer with his country, Cruyff with Feyenoord, Ajax and Barcelona. The other players got older, faded.

The Postmodern Era

In Europe, the axis shifted dramatically to England. The year after Bayern picked up their third successive European Cup, Liverpool picked up its first. In the next eight years, English clubs would contest seven European Cup finals, winning six of them. The Heysel disaster of 1985 ended English club football's epoch of Continental supremacy with their exclusion from European competition. But such unparalleled English success had left its mark on the way the rest of Europe played the game, while leaving English club football locked in a time warp. In the absence of a more cerebral challenge, it seemed that old, unimaginative ways crept back into the game, with an over-emphasis on speed and constant crosses to big centre-forwards. British lack of interest in technical refinement was not a major

1994 Three players, Bruce Grobbelaar, John Fashanu and Hans Segers, were accused of match-fixing. They were eventually cleared

1995 Because of a lengthy legal action by Jean-Marc Bosman, a Belgian player in dispute with his club, the European Court of Justice ruled that existing transfer regulations were a restraint of trade

1996 Manchester United became the first English team to win successive Doubles

1996 Germany won the European championship by beating the Czech Republic 2–1 with a 'Golden goal' in extra time in England

drawback when the British player was stronger and fitter, but with other countries matching British qualities, the domestic game needed to refine itself to catch up. By the time English clubs had returned to European competition, the years of playing only in the wilderness of domestic Cups and Leagues had taken their toll. It took time to get back into the winning groove again.

The type of football that Liverpool had so successfully developed was based on retaining possession with short passes, with the passer moving sharply to be in position for a return pass. In training, the Liverpool players would practise inside a small, semi-enclosed walled box, hitting the ball at an angle and running on to the rebound. This 'faultless' football was one way of re-interpreting Reep's long-ball theory and his study of 'accidental happenings'. Now the ball would be worked into the target area but by fast, accurate, short passing combinations and not the big boot: because retaining possession was crucial to Liverpool's style of play, it was the other side's errors that would cost them dear. However, rather like Holland and Total Football, the success of the system did depend on having a significant number of world-class players at your disposal. And Liverpool could call on the likes of Kevin Keegan, Ray Clemence, Alan Hansen, Graeme Souness, Kenny Dalglish, etc.

But more generally, the English club system that had confounded European opposition in the late 1970s and early 1980s – 4–4–2 – was little different from Ramsey's 1970 England national side. There might be a winger, or not, but there would hardly ever be two. The full-backs were frequently expected to overlap, acting as quasi-wingers. There was much use of the offside trap and, as the flat back-four moved

Flat back-four

The major advantage of this defensive system is that it enables you to play an effective offside trap. The four defenders – two centre-backs and two full-backs – stand in a straight line and, when the ball is played by the opposition into the defence's half, they move up as a unit catching an attacker, who has to run to receive the pass, behind the four defenders and therefore offside.

The disadvantage is that all four defenders have to be alert and play as a unit. Any one of them, by delaying for only a split second, can play an attacker onside leaving the goal at his mercy. Now that Fifa have reinterpreted the interpretation of the rule, an attacker has to be clearly between the defender and the defender's goal, and not level with him, as was the case before the 1994 World Cup. Also, opposing players returning from a previous attack in the direction of their half of the pitch can now be deemed to be not in active play, and therefore not offside.

Tony Adams, centre-half for Arsenal and England, here appealing for offside as the team's back-four successfully play the offside trap

up, the midfield would be congested, effectively shortening the pitch. Strong, tall centre-forwards who could head the ball were still the hallmark of the English game. The spine of a good English side – and replicated in other countries – was much as it always had been: a safe pair of hands in goal; a stopping centre-half, or two; a midfielder provider and a midfield destroyer; and a powerful striker.

The Italians, finally eschewing the discredited *catenaccio* – although if they ever got into trouble, they soon remembered how to play something like it – adopted this classical English style, fiddled with it to suit their purposes and their players, and called it the 'pressing game'. The *libero* had not disappeared from the Italian game, but he was rarely deployed in the same, stifling role as in the 1960s and flat back-fours became more common. Under coach Fabio Cappello, Milan played the 'pressing game' and reached five European Cup finals from 1989 to 1995, winning four of them. Juventus played in the next two finals, and were successful in one. English clubs may not have been at the summit of European football, but a part of their basic formula was.

In England, the flat back-four was mutating. Three centre-backs were tried, either with five across the back, three in midfield, a striker in the hole behind the lone front man (the Christmas tree formation) or three at the back, two wing-backs on the flanks in front of them and a split-striker set-up similar to the Christmas tree. Clubs would now vary these formations to cater for a specific type of opposition, or because key players were injured or suspended. The possibilities were endless, as teams crunched the numbers game. On the final weekend of March in 1998, Arsenal played 4–4–1–1 to Sheffield Wednesday's 4–3–3; Barnsley 3–5–2 to Liverpool's

4–4–2; Bolton 3–5–2 to Leicester's 4–5–1; Coventry 4–4–2 to Derby's 3–5–2; Crystal Palace 4–4–2 to Tottenham's 4–4–2; Everton 4–4–2 to Aston Villa's 3–5–2; Manchester United 4–4–2 to Wimbledon's 4–4–2 and Southampton 4–4–2 to Newcastle's 4–1–2–1–1–1.

As more and more talented overseas players flooded into the English game, in particular the Premiership, the level of sophistication in tactics, as well as skill, began to rub off on English club sides. This quiet revolution was accelerated by the appointment of foreign coaches, notably Ruud Gullit and Gianluca Vialli at Chelsea and Arsène Wenger at Arsenal. So Europeanised had the English game become, that it was not deemed out of place to suggest that the Football Association might even appoint a foreigner as England's national coach to replace the departing Terry Venables. Indeed, his eventual successor, Glenn Hoddle, fits that mould better than that of the standard Premiership manager. At the 1998 World Cup finals, Hoddle's England side demonstrated the sophistication and skills to compete at the highest level. Only a moment of petulant stupidity by David Beckham stopped us from discovering how far England could have gone in the tournament and what they could have achieved.

Arsène Wenger typifies the new breed of European manager in the English Premiership. Under Wenger Arsenal won the Double in 1997–8

The offside trap. Just before player A kicks the ball, the opposing back-four move up as a unit leaving the two forwards offside

Player A is level with the defender when the ball is kicked by B. He is onside. If he was slightly further forward, he would be offside

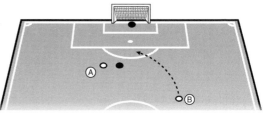

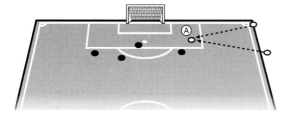

Player A would be offside if the ball was passed forward to him in open play. However, as he has received the ball from either a corner or a throw-in, he is onside

Player A appears to be in an offside position when the ball is kicked. However, as he is not involved in active play, e.g. running back from a previous move or recovering from a painful tackle, he is not offside

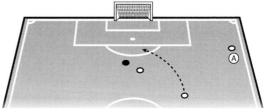

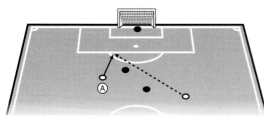

Player A runs forward when the ball is kicked and receives it between the last defender and the goalkeeper. He is onside, as there were two opponents (including the goalkeeper) between him and the goal when the ball was kicked

Player A receives the ball with no defenders between him and the goal. However, he begins his run from his own half and is, therefore, onside

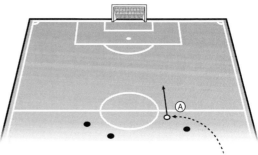

(I) The two attackers are in an onside position waiting for a pass from their midfield

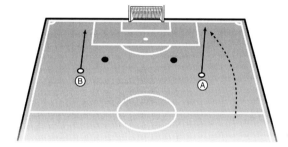

(II) The two attackers run as the ball is kicked over their heads and therefore they are onside

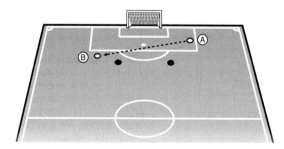

(III) A passes back to B. B remains onside, as the ball has to move forward for an offside to occur

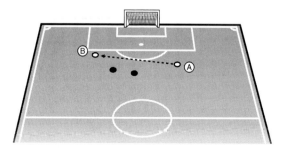

(IV) As A has passed the ball forward, B is offside

Why eleven a side? According to Sepp Blatter, it was because of the English public school system in the mid-nineteenth century where there were ten schoolboys to a dormitory and a schoolteacher in goal.

Pre-1926

This formation is not quite what it seems. The two half-backs were also supposed to be attackers as well as defenders, and the centre-half was a roving, attacking player. The wingers would generally stay on the flanks, providing crosses for the other three forwards. The inside forwards would also be expected to perform defensive duties by dropping back into midfield.

The disadvantage of this formation was the then offside rule of three defenders (one of which would

Pre-1926

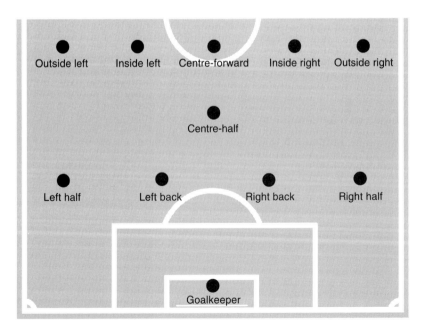

Pre-1926

normally be the goalkeeper) having to be between an attacker and the goal. Newcastle, in particular, exploited this to the hilt by moving defenders up when an attack was mounted, and, with so many offside decisions being given, the Law was changed in 1926 and the number of defenders required for an attacker not to be offside was reduced to two.

Arsenal 1926 Onwards

Nobody had anticipated the dramatic effect the change in the offside rule would have. When the new season opened, defences just couldn't cope and the football results looked more like cricket scores. Arsenal were the first club to crack the new rule and forge a system that is the basis of the modern game. The centre-half would now be a defender instead of a free-ranging attacker, and

Arsenal 1926

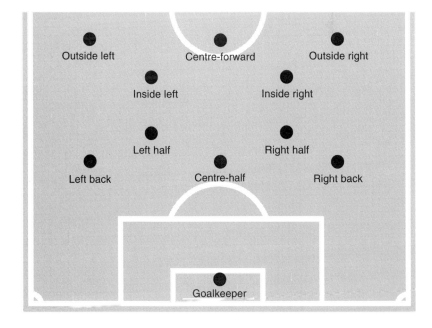

would play a stopping role at the heart of the defence. The wing-halves moved further upfield and the inside-forwards played deeper. Scoring was much more the responsibilty of the centre-forward and the two wingers. The formation was also known as the 'W formation' because of the configuration of the five forwards.

It was a flexible system that combined solid defence with positive attacking potency and Arsenal, under the managership of Herbert Chapman, and then Tom Whittaker, used it to dominate utterly the 1930s.

Brazil 1958

The Brazilians constructed this system to counter the Arsenal-style way of playing. The flat back-

Brazil 1958

four included two stopping centre-halves while the two midfielders were playmakers for the four forwards. Brazil unveiled this formation – and Pele – at the World Cup finals in Sweden and stormed through the tournament, becoming the first team to win a World Cup in a continent not their own.

Brazil 1962

This was the system that Brazil, and latterly England, used to win the World Cups of 1962 and 1966. The advantage over the 1958 system was that the midfield was now more combative and could bolster either the attack, or the defence, more fluently with the extra man. However, the Brazilians, being Brazilians, would play with at least one winger and the third man in midfield would be a converted forward. With that kind of

Brazil 1962

personnel, the system could quickly mutate to 4–2–4. England, on the other hand, played without a real winger and stuck more rigidly to the formation.

Catenaccio

While the rest of the world were emulating the various post-1926 systems, Italy had stubbornly not evolved. When they did, they came up with the most defensive system ever created. The 'sweeper' is precisely that. His job is to cover any mistakes made by the four defenders in front of him. Played with three forwards, the system does have some attacking possibilities. Played with two – the other forward now playing in midfield – the system could be utterly stifling. Inter Milan, under Helenio Herrera, were the arch-exponents, and won two European Cups in the 1960s playing ultra-defensive football.

Catenaccio

Forward winger   Centre-forward   Forward winger

Left half   Right half

Left back   Centre-back   Centre-back   Right back

Sweeper
(libero)

Goalkeeper

The Dutch and the Germans modified the system by treating the sweeper – or *libero*, the free man – as precisely that: free to roam, to attack. Franz Beckenbauer gets most of the credit for turning *catenaccio* on its head and liberating football from its self-imposed sterility.

4–4–2, 4–4–1–1, 3–5–2

All of these systems should be seen as variations of each other. The two things they all have in common is a strike-force of two and a packed defensive strategy that has attacking possibilities. The most adventurous is 4–4–2 depending on which type of player is picked in the four-man midfield; 4–4–2 can be seen as an evolution from 4–3–3. This was inevitable once defence became ever more important in the modern game.

4–4–2 (The striker drops back as shown for 4–4–1–1)

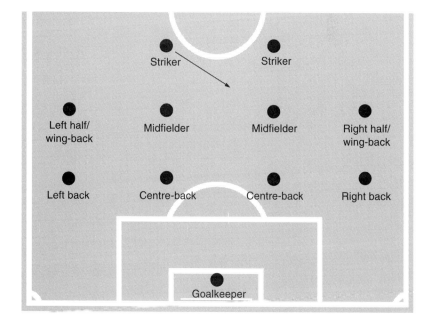

However, neither of the other two formations is defensive *per se*. At first glance, 3–5–2 would appear to be the most conservative, but if the two 'defensive' players on the flanks are speedy, attack-minded defenders, such as Brazil's Roberto Carlos or Italy's Paolo Maldini, then such a formation is primed for rapid counter-attack. With the 3–5–2 system, a team can also play with three 'zonal' defenders or two man-markers and a sweeper.

With 4–4–1–1, the accent is on defending in midfield while being primed for the midfield counter-attack. Nowadays, most Premiership teams can play any of these three systems and they choose which one to play depending on the style of their opponents and the players they have at their disposal.

3–5–2

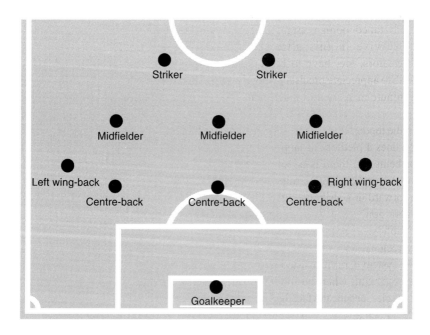

Striker   Striker

Midfielder   Midfielder   Midfielder

Left wing-back

Centre-back   Centre-back   Centre-back   Right wing-back

Goalkeeper

A football match lasts ninety minutes. In that time, an outfield player may have possession of the ball for three minutes. Given that he will play, at most, two matches a week and could earn up to £20,000 a week, that's around £3,000 a minute to justify his job by doing something with the ball when he's got it. And mostly what he does is give it to somebody else – preferably a teammate. This is the heartbeat of football. The pass.

Accurate passing achieves one of the primary objectives of football: the opposition cannot score while your team retains possession of the ball. A pass that gains territorial advantage, whether in yards gained or positional advantage, increases the possibility of your team scoring, another primary objective. However, as the most frequent score of a modern professional football match drifts inexorably from 2–1 towards 1–0, these possibilities are dwindling. This makes intelligent, finely-tuned football essential for any club wishing to survive in this ultra-sophisticated era. Spectators, too, have to be sophisticates if they wish to appreciate precisely what it is these £3,000-a-minute men are doing out there.

In the modern game, a number of systems abound. As does a plethora of jargon. Do not be confused or bemused: there is no such thing as the 'right' system or the 'right' terminology. You can call him a forward or a striker – suffice to say, his job is to score goals, whatever title you give him. Some coaches, Johann Cruyff when he was with Barcelona, for example, will make the players fit the system. Cruyff insisted on using Gary Lineker on the wing when he inherited him from Terry Venables, despite the fact that the only thing Lineker could actually do was score. Shortly afterwards

Lineker moved to Spurs. And scored a hatful of goals. Other coaches adapt the system to suit the players in their squad. So, if, as a coach, you had Teddy Sheringham and a traditional centre-forward as your strike force, you would play Sheringham as a 'split-striker' behind him. Unless you were Cruyff. The debate over 'systems versus players' is really an old chestnut. A good system with the right players will generally beat no system with great players. And a great system with the wrong players will probably beat nobody.

Open Play

The key to unpicking what tactics a team are playing – and why – can often be found in the formation and personnel of the midfield. This is the most crucial part of the pitch, and where the game is usually won or lost. Simply, the midfield is the connection between the defence and the attack; it provides the forwards with the service they need and seeks to prevent the opposition making too many forays into its own half of the field. This dual role demands multi-skilled midfielders and/or specialists. These could be neat passers of the ball; goal-scoring midfielders who make late, dashing runs into the penalty area like David Platt; ball-winners; enforcers with ferocious tackles such as Paul Ince; holders of the ball who wait while teammates adjust their formation to mount an attack; or players who can pick up the ball, attack the opposition and hopefully wreak havoc like Steve McManaman.

In the British game, it is likely that there will be four in the midfield, in a 4–4–2 formation. But whether they play four in a line or with two players wide and with one ahead and one behind (a diamond configuration) will depend on the types of players at the coach's disposal. A midfielder who could combine all of the skills outlined in the previous paragraph seldom comes along. Manchester United's Duncan Edwards probably had more credentials than most; Bryan Robson would be another candidate for Mr Superman. But in general, teams are built around a blend of players that, added together, deliver the necessary composite. However, whether a midfielder is more of a creative player, or more of destroyer, there is one skill they must all have: the ability to pass the ball successfully. This becomes even more important when you realise that in the modern game, the midfield is the most congested part of the pitch.

If the system is 3–5–2, the five midfielders, while

Bryan Robson (right), here with Manchester United, was probably the most complete midfield player of his generation

still being the glue that binds the team, have even more work to do as their defensive responsibilities increase. The three defenders will be centre-backs and, as a consequence, the two wide men in midfield will have to double as wingers and full-backs, hence the term wing-backs. Thus, wing-backs are both attackers and defenders. They must be fast, fit and full of stamina. The remaining three midfielders will almost certainly play in the diamond configuration. The delightful advantage of the 3–5–2 system is that it can be equally effective as an attacking formation – two rampaging wingers – or a defensive one – a game-stifling midfield.

This dichotomy with the midfield – attack meshed with defence – is always at the nerve centre of a match. Frequently goals are conceded by an error in the midfield. With defences so regimented and organised, it is the 'surprise' attack in front of the defence that causes it to break down. And, of course, the reverse is true. Midfield players often get almost as many goal-scoring opportunities as strikers. The surprise element – a well-timed, late run into the area from the midfield – is very difficult to defend against, particularly because the defence will be spending most of its time trying to nullify the opposing pair of strikers.

The facility of midfield players to sway the course of the game is partly to do with the British game's obsession with zonal marking. On the Continent, the tendency is for man-to-man marking, where each player has an allotted player and sticks to him. The back-up to this quasi-robotic system is the *libero*, the sweeper who's there to mop up any problems that arise. Such a system makes the game slower, as the two sides probe each other with short passes and darting runs, trying to detect a weakness. In Britain, the sweeper system is generally an alien addendum to the lexicon of the football language. Instead, British defenders tend to mark space and are therefore only responsible for a player when he enters their zone. If the attacker shifts to another zone, then he becomes the other defender's responsibility. If a team is playing 4–4–2, then the zones are simple to visualise. The defending half is divided into four equal vertical zones between the goal-line and the half-way line with the full-backs covering their quarters on the flank, and the centre-backs covering the middle two quarters.

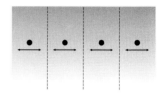

Zonal marking. Each player in the back four controls his own area

It's easy to see, then, that as an attacker moves from one zone to another, other attackers adding to the onslaught could easily bemuse a unit of four defenders as they twist and turn, quickly calculating which player is their responsibility. If this happens in the target area of their own goal, the defender will tend to stick with 'his man'. This, unless the midfield is quick to respond to its defensive chores, could be devastating. If the defensive unit is pulled out of shape because a defender has to follow his man – who will probably be in possession of the ball – holes can appear in the defence. Other defenders may be decoyed away from their zone and further gaps might emerge. These chinks may be cruelly exploited by late runs from the attacking midfielders when, and if, the ball is crossed, or passed, into those danger areas.

The weakness of this system is that the defence can be caught 'square' by attackers drawing them out of position, leaving gaps which can be exploited

Defenders will often use their position to 'show' an attacker with ball into a part of the field they believe is less dangerous. They can show him the outside by cutting off the inside, or vice versa. The idea is block off whatever is deemed to be the danger zone by making space available

Although often used as an out-and-out striker for his country, Holland, Dennis Bergkamp's preferred role is as a 'split' striker, a role he performs with devastating effect for Arsenal

The defenders are 'showing' player A, a good crosser of the ball, into a central position so that he can't cross. The other defenders are forcing player B, a goal-scoring centre-forward, out to the wing to lessen his view of goal. The disadvantage for the defence is that space is thereby created for other players to make runs

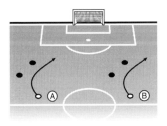

elsewhere. A team with a solid centre would tend to show an opponent with the ball on the wing the inside, especially if they know he is an excellent crosser of the ball. Teams that feel comfortable with crosses and have speedy full-backs would tend to show the outside and 'push' him further down the flank. One of the dangers with showing the inside is the possibility of giving away free-kicks within shooting range, or penalties. This is particularly perilous when the attacker is known to have a sudden change of pace, or worse, an eye for goal. The attacker, with the ball on the defender's blind-side, will take him into an area that commits him to a challenge, accelerate – knowing full well the defender won't get the ball – and let the defender take the man, not the ball. It has been suggested that this is a sophisticated form of diving, and some referees treat it as such, others don't. Whatever one's view of this ploy, this aspect of modern play has tested the competency of referees more than any other.

Although the standard British defence is a flat back-four, the attacking formation they seek to blunt varies quite considerably. They could be facing a lone striker with five in midfield; twin strikers with another behind them – 'in the hole'; or 'split' twin strikers. Each poses different problems. In theory, the lone striker should be the easiest to contain but, in practice, those teams who play this formation must have a strong, fast and alert forward who will also be good in the air. A stream of midfield players coming down the flanks, or through the centre, while the lone striker twists and feints, trying to lure the defence out of position, is as problematical as defending against two conventional forwards. The man 'in the hole' and 'split' striker formations ask different questions. In each case, the player in the deeper position will still be too forward for the defending midfielders and, in a swift movement, can become an unmarked 'spare' man up front or, if he has attracted the attention of the defence, quickly release the ball for the other forward(s) to run on to.

This is why the defensive responsibilities of the midfield, dovetailing with the defence, are so important. For the forwards to function properly they need two things: service from their teammates and space to operate. If the midfield

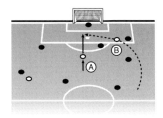

The striker B heads the ball into the box where it is met by the 'split' striker A, who has been lurking between the midfield and the defence and has moved too quickly for either to handle

can cut off the distribution, and the defence can deny the strikers the space they need, then the opposition will find it difficult to create many goal-scoring opportunities. And the fewer the opportunities, the fewer goals they will score. Obviously there have been games won with a solitary shot on goal in the entire ninety minutes, but they are few and far between. Generally, the number of goals scored is proportional to the number of chances they make. This is why most teams operate a 'shoot on sight' policy, even if, to the spectator, the probability of the ball actually entering the net seems extremely low.

Another reason for speculative shooting is the uncertainty factor. The ball may take a deflection or swerve deceptively in the air; the goalkeeper may make an error – drop the ball, palm it into his own net etc., you may get a corner, a free-kick or a penalty as the defence panics. It is a truism that if you don't buy a ticket, you can't win the lottery. It is the same with scoring: if you don't shoot, you won't score.

There are also psychological advantages in shooting on sight. If the defence and the midfield believe that a shot can come at any time, and from anywhere, then they may tend to mark too tightly. Ironically, it can be easier for the player with the ball to beat his man the closer he is to him. Also, if the player marks too tightly, he can be easier to lure out of position. A professional striker only needs half-a-yard of space to score and, as the defence loses its shape, such holes might open up. Shooting on sight also means the ball is where you want it to be, heading towards their goal, not yours. The alternative options, passing or trying to beat your marker, always carry the risk of losing possession which, if a concerted attack is being mounted, open up the danger of a quick counter-attack. Giving away the ball just outside the opposition's penalty area can be a very expensive thing to do, as an astute passer could unleash his strikers at the other end in the twinkling of an eye.

Penalties

Defending at set-pieces (penalties, free-kicks, throw-ins and corners) poses a different set of problems from open play. Penalties are not as straightforward as they may appear. First, the goalkeeper no longer has to be motionless on his goal-line and can move laterally. So, if they wish, keepers are at liberty to attempt to distract the penalty-taker and break his concentration. As approximately three-quarters of penalties are successful, the psychological burden lies more with

Eric Cantona (No 7) sends the Chelsea keeper the wrong way from the penalty spot in Manchester United's 4–0 1994 Cup final win over Chelsea

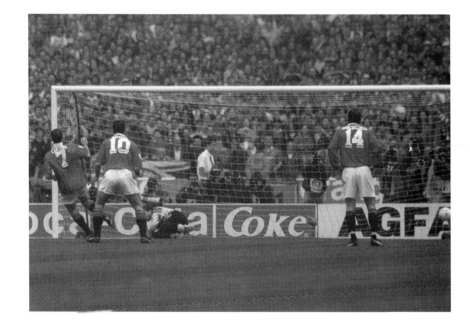

the penalty-taker than the keeper. Consequently, many keepers decide to dive to one side or another before, or just as, the ball is kicked, hoping that this gives them a 50 per cent chance of saving it. However, some penalty-takers respond by shooting straight down the middle to the very spot where the keeper was before he dived, thus cancelling out the 50–50 calculation made by the keeper. Also, penalty-takers can feint to take a shot, briefly pause, and, having seen which way the keeper has dived, put the ball into the other side of the net. The basic options for the penalty-taker are simple: pace or place. Wallop the ball in the general direction of the goal or take careful aim at the space inside one or other of the two posts and fire. Which one they choose depends on temperament, what kind of goalkeeper they face and the choice they made the last time they scored a penalty.

The psychological burden on the penalty-taker can be extraordinary. Garth Crooks (former Stoke, Spurs, Manchester United and Charlton forward) described the experience as 'nerve-wracking'. He says he tried to use both pace and place. 'It's the most difficult to achieve', Crooks said, 'but it maximises the chance of scoring. The worst thing is the amount of time you have. I found the longer you have the worse it is. It's like a golfer when it comes to putting, like getting the yips.' Odd things can go through a player's mind. Many people believe that West Ham made an error of judgement when they allowed John Hartson to take a penalty against Arsenal at Highbury in 1998. Facing him was David Seaman, a player whom Hartson would have idolised when he was a young player at Arsenal. For those watching, it seemed that the West Ham striker was simply intimidated by the situation. Not surprisingly, Hartson made a botch of it.

Although no players other than the goalkeeper and the penalty-taker are allowed inside the penalty area, the other players will not be passive spectators. If the keeper does save the ball, there is every possibility of a rebound – either for the defence or the attack. Both sets of players will be aware of this and take up positions around the area accordingly.

In the modern game, the penalty has grown to be more and more important as defences leak fewer goals, the rules favouring the attacker are strengthened and the Thespian abilities of diving forwards dramatically improve. And with the penalty shoot-out the now customary solution to draws in Cup competitions, both keepers and outfield players are – or should be – honing their spotkick skills. However, it does seem patently ludicrous that the climax of the most important competition on earth – the World Cup final – should eventually be decided by the lottery of a penalty shoot-out, as it was in the United States in 1994. An alternative solution, the so-called 'Golden goal' – a misleading sobriquet for sudden death in extra time after ninety minutes are played – was tried out in the European championships in England in 1996 and, like the penalty shoot-out two years earlier, determined the outcome of the tournament in the showpiece final (see next page).

Matches in Cup competitions, by definition, eventually have to have a winner. If, after ninety minutes, the scores are level, then the two teams generally replay on the away team's ground. If, after ninety minutes in the second match, the scores are still level, then thirty minutes of extra time are played in two halves of fifteen minutes. If this fails to break the deadlock, then there is a penalty shoot-out in which each team has five penalty attempts. But, unlike penalties in normal play, the ball becomes 'dead' when the outcome of the kick is clear, i.e. the kicker can not kick the ball again if it rebounds to him.

The five players are nominated, in rotation, before the penalties are taken. If the scores are level after all ten penalties are completed, each side takes another penalty in turn until one side fails to score. The original ten penalty-takers are not permitted to take another penalty until their six teammates – if necessary – have taken theirs. No substitutions are allowed; only the twenty-two players on the pitch at the final whistle are eligible to take the penalties.

Golden Goal

At the 1996 European championship finals, Fifa permitted Uefa to experiment with the 'Golden goal' in the knock-out phase of the tournament. Instead of playing extra time for the full thirty minutes, it would be a period of 'sudden death' whereby the first team to score would be declared the winner. If no team scored in the thirty minutes then penalties would be used as in the normal penalty shoot-out to decide the outcome. Ironically the only match that was resolved by sudden-death overtime was the final when Germany beat the

Czech Republic 2–1 with a controversial goal in the fifth minute of extra time. Under the previous rules, the Czechs would have had twenty-five minutes to recover. It was a terrible anti-climactic ending to the tournament.

Like many rule changes, the 'Golden goal' had precisely the opposite effect from that which the organisers had intended. The 'Golden goal' could have resolved four of the six knock-out matches before the final. Instead, all four went to penalties. The 'Golden goal' was supposed to encourage attacking play in extra time but, because the result was on a knife edge, most of the teams played more cautiously. Despite the apparent failure of this experiment, Fifa stubbornly persisted with it for the 1998 World Cup finals.

The German team celebrate Bierhoff's winning Golden goal while the Czechs slump to the ground in despair

Away Goals

In two legged European ties, such as the knock-out phase of the European Cup, away goals are used to decide the winner when the aggregate scores are level. So, if a team loses 2–1 away and wins 1–0 at home, that team goes through by virtue of their away goal. If the away-goal rule does not break the deadlock, then extra time and the penalty shoot-out apply. The away goal has a profound affect on the tactics of teams involved in European competition and can confuse spectators.

Television commentators often say that away goals count 'double'; while this is true, in a sense, it is also potentially misleading. Away goals only count double *when the aggregate scores are level* and not when they are unequal. The impact of conceding goals at home can have the most extraordinary effect in the return match. For example, say team X lost 2–1 away and were winning 1–0 at home. As the scores stand, team X would win because the aggregate score is 2–2 and, with their away goal counting double, the score is *notionally* 3–2 to team X. Now, if team Z score, the aggregate score is 2–3 and team Z would go through. If team X now score again, the aggregate score would be 3–3 and, as team X's and team Z's away goals are identical – one apiece – extra time and a penalty shoot-out loom.

But this is a high-scoring match – and team Z stun team X by finding the net again. The aggregate score is 3–4 and team X now have real problems. There is only one way to win the tie – they have to score twice before the ninety minutes are up. There is no possibility of extra time, because team X can never match, or supersede, team Z's two away goals. If team X score just once more, the aggregate scores will once again be level, but team Z will prevail by virtue of their two away goals to team X's one.

Free-kicks

The direct free-kick, too, has mushroomed in importance in the modern game, especially those that are within shooting range, which today means within 30–35 yards from the goal. If it is in shooting range then the defending side will, under the guidance of the goalkeeper scuttling along his line to check the angles, form a human 'wall' ten yards between the ball and their goal. Generally nine of the ten outfield players will take up defensive roles – leaving one striker upfield in case of a breakaway. The number of players in the wall (mostly forwards and midfielders) will be a function of the distance and the angle of the kick. The nearer the free-kick and the flatter the angle, the more players there will be in the wall. The attacking side may try to disrupt this wall, by

Roberto Carlos, left wing-back for Brazil and Real Madrid, is probably the world's leading free-kick specialist

1) A skilful free-kick specialist, such as Chelsea's Zola (A) or Arsenal's Bergkamp (C), can bend or swerve a ball around or over the defensive wall. David Beckham's perfectly-judged goal against Columbia in the 1998 World Cup finals is an example of shot B

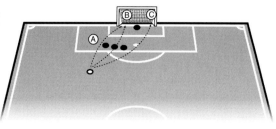

2) An attacking player has positioned himself at the edge of the wall. As the free-kick is being taken, he suddenly peels away, leaving a gap for the kicker to exploit.

3) A carefully worked-out free-kick, demonstrated by Argentina for their second goal against England in the 1998 World Cup finals. Batistuta (A) makes a dummy run over the ball, his teammate Veron (B) runs on to it and passes to Zanetti

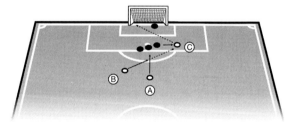

(C) who has run from the wall to receive the ball. Unmarked, and with space, he does not waste the opportunity. Thomas Brolin scored a similar goal for Sweden in the 1994 World Cup finals

4) A: An unmarked player arrives to the kicker's right and the kicker passes to him. He shoots before the defence has time to re-organise. B: Also used when the free-kick is close to goal and more distance is required for the shot. Holland's Ronald Koeman was an exponent of the latter

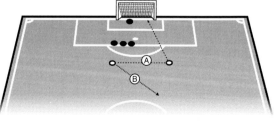

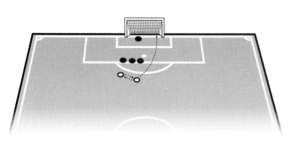

5) The kicker stands beside a teammate who passes the ball back immediately to the kicker, who shoots towards the goal

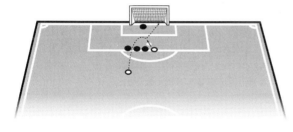

6) This is an increasingly-used ploy. A teammate stands in or at the edge of the wall. The kicker lobs the ball over the head of the defence to his teammate who has spun round to face the goal. Japan used this one against Croatia in the 1998 World Cup finals but failed to capitalise on it

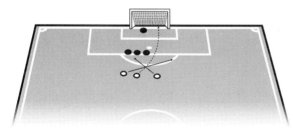

7) Three or four players stand close to the ball and make dummy runs in different directions until it is kicked. This can confuse the wall and the goalkeeper

8) In this example, the kicker flicks the ball up to a teammate who shoots on the volley. A Matt le Tissier special

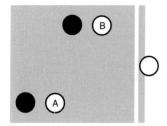

Players A and B wait for a throw-in.

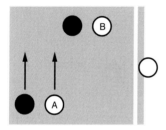

A makes a run toward B, taking his marker with him

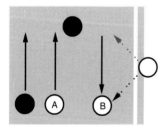

B then runs, leaving his marker undecided, and picks the ball up in space

introducing some of their own players into it, or forming their own smaller version of the wall immediately in front of it. The former ploy is to create a 'hole' in the wall by an attacking player moving out of the way when the ball is kicked. The latter is to obscure from the wall exactly what trickery the kicker may be employing. The kicker may opt to blast the ball through the wall; pass it laterally to a player whose sight of goal is not obscured by the wall; confuse the defence as to who is taking the ball, and therefore in what direction the ball will travel; chip the ball over the wall for an attacker, or attackers, to sneak in and score; and lastly bend the ball over, or around, the wall into either of the top corners by the posts.

Free-kicks well outside shooting range used to be seen as just a stop–start form of open play. Nowadays, the game has so developed that any set-piece in the attacking half of the field can be dangerous. Quickly-taken ones can kick-start a swift attack with the equivalent of an incisive pass; more measured ones are frequently lofted over midfield towards the target area.

Throw-ins

Throw-ins, unless a team has a long-throw specialist, are much the same as short free-kicks and are usually taken quickly. Procrastination by the thrower can lead to his discovering that everybody is marked – remember his team is down to ten men while he is taking the throw. The Leeds team under Don Revie in the late 1960s and 1970s had turned this into an art-form and frequently opposition players poised to take a throw-in would be unable to find a free man. Long-throw specialists are precisely that, and can project the ball prodigious distances but without much power. They are especially dangerous when throw-ins are given near the corner flag and the ball will probably be hurled into the mêlée of the six-yard box, rather like a cross from the byline or a corner-kick. Dummy runs will often be made in these dead ball situations as players seek to decoy players out of position.

Corners

Corners should be more dangerous than they are in practice, given that, until the ball is touched by the attacking side, you can't be offside. However, corners rarely produce as many goals as free-kicks within shooting range, which is why any free-kick is taken seriously. This is generally because of the

Oman-Biyik of Cameroon flicks on a corner at the near post during his country's 1–0 defeat of Argentina in the 1990 World Cup finals

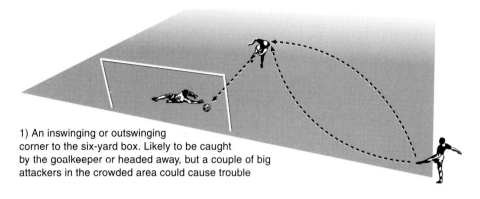

1) An inswinging or outswinging
corner to the six-yard box. Likely to be caught
by the goalkeeper or headed away, but a couple of big
attackers in the crowded area could cause trouble

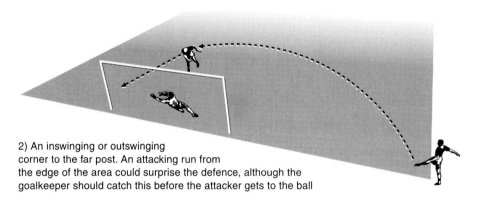

2) An inswinging or outswinging
corner to the far post. An attacking run from
the edge of the area could surprise the defence, although the
goalkeeper should catch this before the attacker gets to the ball

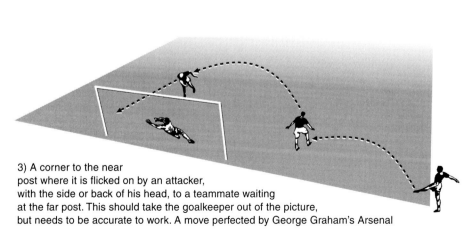

3) A corner to the near
post where it is flicked on by an attacker,
with the side or back of his head, to a teammate waiting
at the far post. This should take the goalkeeper out of the picture,
but needs to be accurate to work. A move perfected by George Graham's Arsenal

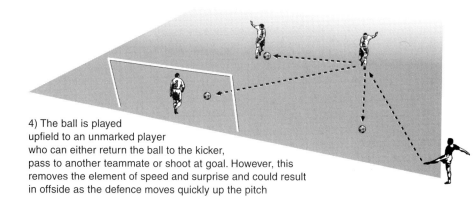

4) The ball is played
upfield to an unmarked player
who can either return the ball to the kicker,
pass to another teammate or shoot at goal. However, this
removes the element of speed and surprise and could result
in offside as the defence moves quickly up the pitch

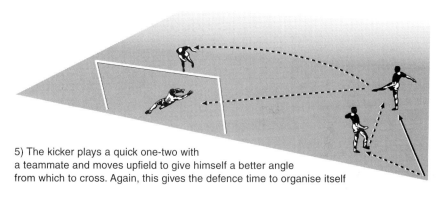

5) The kicker plays a quick one-two with
a teammate and moves upfield to give himself a better angle
from which to cross. Again, this gives the defence time to organise itself

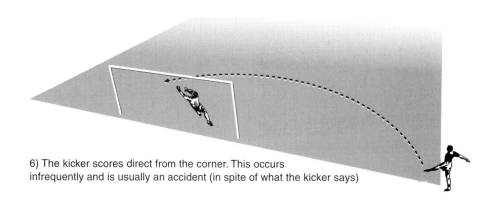

6) The kicker scores direct from the corner. This occurs
infrequently and is usually an accident (in spite of what the kicker says)

narrowness of the angle, the paucity of options open to the corner-taker, and the fact that defences have been dealing with corners since time immemorial: defending against 'mock' corners is one of the most well-rehearsed drills on the training ground.

In essence, there are a limited number of corners: an inswinging corner to either the far post or the six-yard box; an outswinging corner to the near post or the six-yard box; a short-corner to a nearby teammate; or a pull-back to the outside of the penalty area where a player will suddenly make himself free for an unexpected shot. As the defending team will not know which corner is coming, the basic defence is identical. A man will be stationed on each post and, as best they can in a fluid, volatile and crowded penalty area, mark all the opposing players. Near-post corners are looking for a flick-on, either to the far post where strikers will be lurking, or the six-yard box. Inswinging, far-post corners are an invitation for the goalkeeper to come off his line to try to catch, or clear, the ball. If he fails, his goal is extremely vulnerable.

Corners into the centre of the six-yard box test the quickness of everybody's reflexes, with a marginal advantage to the attacking side as they are more likely to be facing the right way. But, generally, defenders do expect that their goalkeeper will catch, or punch, any corner played into the six-yard box. And if the goalkeeper is confident enough, he should collect the ball. Short-corners, balls played to a teammate downfield, but only a few yards away, are rarely successful; while they do widen the angle on goal, they also give the defence the option to step up and play the offside trap, something the very best defences can do.

Scoring First

The importance of scoring first cannot be overstated. In the early 1960s an analysis of over 1,000 matches showed that home teams who took the lead first only lost approximately 10 per cent of those games. For away teams the figure was understandably higher, around 25 per cent. And, despite the changing nature of the game, those figures are remarkably similar today. An analysis by the *Independent* in late 1997 of Premiership matches from 1995 showed that in 1995–6, 69 per cent of games were won by teams scoring first, 20 per cent were drawn and 11 per cent lost. In the following season the figures were 67 per cent won, 23 per cent drawn and 10 per cent lost. And by December 1997, the trend was much the same, with 72 per cent winning, 17 per cent drawing and 11 per cent losing. Not surprisingly, the team with the best record for capitalising on drawing first blood is Manchester United. According to the *Independent*'s survey, in 217 Premiership matches United had not lost a game – home or away – in which they scored first.

The Way the Game has Changed

Recently retired professional footballers say they are told by the current crop of players that the modern game is quicker these days and is one of the reasons why skill and ability is declining. This quicker pace also means that players have to be fitter than even a few years ago, particularly with the evolution of defensive strategies which condense the playing area as defending players push up into midfield. If both sides are at it, which is more and more the case, the actual playing area can be as small as twenty-five yards. The

Channels

A number of casual football fans howl and blame the passer when they see an angled pass into the opposing team's territory go wildly astray. Quite often, it may not be his fault at all and the blame should be given to the player for whom the pass was intended. The passer has played the ball into space behind a defender, or defenders, with the expectation that his teammate will run into that 'channel', usually an imaginary diagonal. If the player for whom the pass is intended does not spot the 'channel', or mistimes his run, then the pass will fail.

A number of passes have to be played into space, rather than directly to the player, because not only would it be a much easier task for a defender to mark the recipient, but the possibility of an interception increases alarmingly. And, an interception could easily lead to a swift counter-attack that could prove costly as the passer's teammates are likely to be caught out of position.

'squeeze', as it is known, had a profound effect on managers and coaches, as they had to re-think the functions of their players. For example, to beat the offside trap nowadays, strikers have to find ways to bring their midfield players into the game. Mark Hughes's ability to hold the ball up, while other players arrive, is one way of doing it.

A striking difference between the way the game is played now and, say half-a-dozen years ago, is the role demanded of goalkeepers. With the bulk of play in a narrow segment of the midfield, goalkeepers have to patrol the areas behind defences and not just the penalty area, or the six-yard box, as they used to do. Now the goalkeeper also has to play a type of sweeping role, similar to a *libero*, over and above his traditional duties. If you go back to the eras of Gordon Banks, Peter

England goalkeeper Ray Clemence rarely moved far from his goal line. Modern keepers, such as Manchester United's Peter Schmeichel, frequently venture out of their penalty areas to initiate attacks

Shilton and Ray Clemence – three of the world's greatest keepers – they would never have been expected to perform such a role, and they wouldn't necessarily have been comfortable with it. But the best keepers today are. Clemence, in particular, didn't like coming out of his six-yard box, never mind his area.

Although fans do not like the negativity of the modern game, the adoption of the squeeze was inevitable, given that the trajectory of most professional sports is to accentuate defence. Simply, the squeeze denies players space, and does it in a sophisticated manner. And if you deny players space, even good players, you pose them problems.

The efficacy of the squeezing game depends on consistency throughout the team. It is crucial for the team to play as a strategic unit. Once the squeeze is working, the players start to hunt in packs, and normally this starts from the front, with the strikers and the midfielders. So, when the opposition are in possession of the ball on, say, the left-hand side of the field, one, two, perhaps three players will arrive to deny that particular space and force the opposition to transfer the ball to another area, rather than make a significant advance upfield. The opposition may lose possession because of this harassment, or they may not. But if they retain possession, they still should not have made any significant advance and will have simply moved their problem from one place to another. Where there will be another little pack hunting to win the ball back.

For this strategy to work, footballers have had to abandon any notion of playing traditional roles in

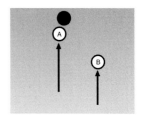

Player A, a winger, has the ball and player B, his full back, is running up the touchline and about to pass the two players. The defender now has two options

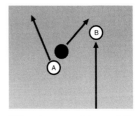

Either he moves to mark B, and A turns infield with the ball, retaining possession

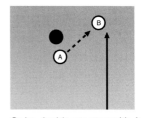

Or he decides to stay with A, who passes to B and an attack is on

This is a difficult dilemma for the defender and a useful attacking move

conventional positions. For example, strikers have also to be defenders, and learn how to defend from the front. Ian Rush was one of the first forwards to master this art when he was at Liverpool, and, in doing so, helped to transform the English striker's game. An art that Mark Hughes was still pursuing at Chelsea in 1998.

This is how Rush did it. If an opposition full-back had the ball at his feet, in the full-back position, hoping to play the killing ball to a striker down the line, the first person he would be confronted by was Rush. The striker's prime intention would be straightforward: to get a block on the ball, put it out of play and force the opposition to take a throw-in deep in their own half. His secondary intention would be to put the full-back under pressure, deny him space, close him down and effectively say to the full-back: 'It's going to have to be a great ball,

Ian Rush (left) putting pressure on Everton's Kevin Ratcliffe

isn't it? Forget the ball to your centre-forward, give it to your winger ten yards away. I'm not going to let you make a killer ball. If I can't get my foot in, I'm going to get close enough for you to think about it.' And that might be enough. Better, the stymied full-back could make a hash of the whole thing and lose possession. In the most dangerous area of the pitch – in sight of his own goal.

But the only way Rush can operate effectively is if his team has squeezed up. If they haven't squeezed the opposition, then they're strung out like a line of washing and there will be lots of space around them. In that situation, four defenders can easily play against two strikers all day: they simply play through them. But if they're squeezed up tightly, and Rush and his co-striker are operating as a unit, both of them harrying the defence, two players can close their four defenders down. When somebody like Rush is doing his job, it's a nightmare for defenders.

Midfield players are also frustrated by the squeeze. Their disenchantment comes from the lack of time they now have on the ball. Not only do they feel they are constantly under pressure to make a quick decision, but because the way the field is condensed, the ball can spend a lot of time travelling through the air to outmanoeuvre the opposition. This reduces the number of possibilities midfielders have to influence the outcome of the match. To the spectator, the midfield battle is almost seen in slow-motion compared with the helter-skelter it actually is on the field. Split-second decisions under pressure, that is the job description of the modern midfielder.

Whenever tactics are employed in a game, and they are executed brilliantly by individuals, it gives the opposition immense problems. They say: 'Hang on a second, what's going on here? Why am I not immediately being marked by my opposite number? And the space I expected to have here, I don't. It's 25 yards upfield, but I've got to get past this man here and now, he's in front of me.' It can take an entire first-half for a team to come to terms with the opposition's tactics. Players, even great players, have to adjust to the style of play that they face. And the greater a player they are, the quicker they adjust.

However, English football does not possess enough of those great players who can make such adjustments. What the current tactics demand – if the game is not to become bogged down in tactical

After a long and illustrious playing career, and a spell as chairman of the PFA, Garth Crooks now works as a commentator for TV and radio

sterility – are the kind of Total footballers Ajax and Bayern had in their heyday in the 1970s. Those teams had, for the first time in modern football, players who were comfortable on the ball in any position, who could rotate, causing all sorts of problems all over the pitch. It freaked people when Paul Breitner, a full-back for Bayern, was in the last third of the pitch, in complete control of the ball and totally comfortable on it. Part of the problem with English football, as opposed to the Continental variety, was that it was only in the last twenty years that the need for tactical sophistication took hold, and even then in only a rudimentary fashion.

Garth Crooks can still recall when the scales fell from his eyes: 'I remember playing in Europe for Spurs in the 1980s being told by my coach that if we lost our marker then effectively we'd get punished. Ultimately with a goal. I was incredulous. My marker was a centre-half. Who cares if I lost the centre-half? I was told that if he got beyond me, he could, from the half-way line, put in a killer blow to one of his strikers, or worse, score himself! But we didn't have defenders who could do that with any regularity. We still don't. Liverpool did with Alan Hansen and Forest with Kenny Burns – but he was a former centre-forward. They were the two exceptions. Both of them could murder you. Hansen didn't score many goals, but he could pick out the pass to kill you.'

Because a greater appreciation of the importance of varying tactics came so late to English players, they emerged in an unlikely way, and in an unlikely place. Crooks believes that players became much more aware of specific tactics when Graham Taylor was the manager at Watford and employed a strategy that was unaffectionately called Route One and was akin to Charles Reep's 'long-ball' theory. Players had to analyse why it was so difficult to play against. They hated it because it inhibited the way they wanted to play and disturbed their enjoyment. And it baffled them. They were forced to devise a way of imposing their tactics on teams playing that way. 'Why it became so unpopular was that when Watford had the ball, they didn't have the players with the ability to do something with it that was creative and pleasing to the eye [they hoofed it upfield] – whereas Liverpool did', Crooks said. 'But when Liverpool didn't have the ball, they played much the same way as Watford, they closed down, hunted in packs and forced errors. Arsenal under George Graham did it beautifully. Arsenal came under a lot of criticism because they had players who could play but, because of George, his tactics, and his complete and utter commitment to those tactics, he denied expression to a number of players.'

What Players *Really* Think

Fans do not believe that footballers are ordinary people trying to do a professional job. Most fans believe that they are overpaid and ultimately don't really care enough about the fortunes of the club. And fans do not really grasp that professional footballers got to the top the hard way, by being good enough, and working hard enough, to escape the scrapheap. As many as 50 per cent of those who sign for football clubs at the age of eighteen, drop out by the time they are twenty-one. Another 25 per cent also fall away later and do not make a career out of football. Football is a tough industry, with as tough a standard expected from the customers as that expected by the management.

A pro's complaint would go something like this: 'Real fans don't believe that footballers have a bad day at the office. They won't allow it. What do you mean? You're a footballer and you're paid all this money, and you have a bad day at the office? Come on, you're supposed to be brilliant every match.' There are a host of things that could conspire to create that bad day. Loss of form; niggling injuries; fear of losing your place; problems at home; fear of re-injuring yourself; and all the other stuff that makes up the modern life they share with their spectators. With one exception.

Most fans are extremely unlikely to wake up in the morning and, over a cup of tea and toast, open the papers to read that their employers are head-hunting another person to take their job. That is, in essence, what happens all the time to professional footballers. They read that their club has made a bid for a player who plays in their position. A player who will supposedly be taking their place in the side. Transfer speculation is every professional footballer's nightmare. Imagine what went through Andy Cole's mind when he read that the Chilean *wunderkind*, Marcello Salas, might be going to Old Trafford? It's Tuesday morning, there's a big game on Saturday, Cole hasn't scored recently, what is he thinking about? Meanwhile, he has to prepare himself for the big game on Saturday at Old Trafford.

Players have to live football twenty-four hours a day. You're not allowed to do anything else – even if you wanted to. If you go to a club or a pub, people want to talk football to you. Teammates generally stick together, invariably swapping tales about football, women or worse. Those players who try to get away from it, to rise above this sort of work

Intent

Many people still believe that a foul has to be intentional for a player to be penalised and that this is within the referee's discretion. This is not true – with the one exception of handball, where the game could be reduced to the level of farce by players deliberately kicking the ball at opponents' arms and getting an automatic free-kick, or penalty. Until recent years, referees did have a large degree of discretion at their disposal. However, wishing to harmonise the interpretation of the Laws of the Game, Fifa periodically issue guidelines to referees and also tighten up the Laws. The current tendency is for these instructions and alterations to favour the attacking side and to try to create a more exciting brand of football.

clique, or shopfloor chat, are generally seen as being arrogant, aloof, snobbish. Art galleries? Read quality broadsheets? Go to the theatre, the ballet, opera ... forget it! This kind of attitude has been the bane of *Guardian*-reading Graeme Le Saux's life and allegedly one of the reasons behind his brawl with teammate David Batty on the pitch in the European Champions League match for Blackburn against Spartak Moscow in 1995. There have been other gifted players who did not fit the stereotype. Pat Nevin and Brian McClair are two examples; Others include Osvaldo Ardiles, who studied law, and Socrates, the Brazilian captain in 1982, a qualified doctor.

However incestuous players constantly socialising with their teammates might appear, most pros will tell you it's essential in building team spirit and ironing out problems. When Roberto Mancini moved to Lazio in 1997, having spent virtually all

Socrates of Brazil, a qualified doctor and inspirational captain

of his career at Sampdoria, he was very surprised that his new teammates didn't frequently go out to restaurants together and talk. After an early-season run of indifferent results, Mancini suggested that the players sort things out over the dinner table, and on a regular basis. A spectacular, unbeaten run followed, as Lazio surged up the League table and captured their first Italian Cup in forty years – having knocked out Juventus in the semi-final. The Roman club also reached the Uefa Cup final.

Lazio were unusual. Most players will tell you that they couldn't think of a team they've played for where such regular social contact between teammates didn't happen. It also helps to clear the air, to sort out whatever problems, egos, there are. Occasionally it might erupt into a flashpoint, things are said out in the open, tempers flare, blows might be exchanged. But the players tend to see it as a problem sorted out, as if the festering sore has been lanced. And that kind of private confrontation is welcomed in the game, it's seen as therapeutic. The public are outraged, the media have a field day, players are fined and admonished, but, privately, inside the game, it's seen as healthy and productive. The administrators just wish the media hadn't found out about it. (They don't always.)

Football is a physical game and aggression is an essential element. If a professional snarls at you on the pitch, you are supposed to snarl back. To do their job properly, footballers have to be committed, both mentally and athletically. This commitment can't just be switched off, whether you are on the ball or off the ball, running into position or tackling. But, although professionals pride themselves on football being a man's game, they draw the line at deliberately trying to injure an opponent, to get them

Diving

Throwing oneself dramatically to the ground in the penalty area in response to an opponent's challenge – whether real or not – in an attempt to gain a penalty. This has always been a feature of some forwards' play – Manchester City's Francis Lee was constantly accused of it. In the Premiership in recent years, 'diving' seems to be on the increase with the influx of foreign players. Jurgen Klinsmann had a notorious reputation for 'diving' in England, something that he was unaware of until a friend told him about it before his arrival at Spurs. At the press conference to announce his transfer, Klinsmann neatly took the sting out of his poor reputation by inquiring of the journalists: 'Where is the nearest diving school?' And when he scored his first goal for Spurs, he and his teammates all swallow-dived on to the ground in celebration. This gimmick has been copied around the world.

sent off, or booked. There is an unwritten, private code, a spirit of the game, that all professionals share. Ironically, the penalty for breaking this code – cheating – will be punished on the pitch by actions such as trying to get the culprit penalised by the referee with a caution or a dismissal. Players who habitually cheat are shunned. They are the black sheep of the family.

Fans are another part of this family of football, but are probably not as important to their team's performance as they might think. Privately, some older professionals say that in their younger days the crowd was very important to them, but they grew out of it. In a sense, they had to. Garth Crooks explained it this way: 'When you see your fans there waiting as the coach arrives, taking up the side of a stadium, it's very exhilarating. In 1981, I remember at Hillsborough [Spurs versus Wolves in the FA Cup semi-final] walking out at 2pm on to the pitch and thinking: this is unbelievable. Those thoughts and feelings change at 3pm. Because I'm working.

'In Barcelona in 1982, on the morning of the match [European Cup Winners Cup semi-final], we went to the Nou Camp for a training session. There were Spurs fans there waiting for us, it was a big lift, a huge one. It's terribly important in Europe, where you feel more isolated, because you really are on foreign territory. To see your people there, they do become part of the battle, but again the complexion changes. When you play, you adopt a different view. It changes again at the end of the game when you see them there. It changes dramatically if they've misbehaved, if your fans have been involved in violence or have clashed with police. You almost look at them and say, I don't want anything to do with these people.'

Dribbling

This is running with the ball close to the feet; by twisting and turning with the ball, feinting with the upper body, the player in possession attempts to evade opponents' tackles. Any list of the most memorable dribbling moments must include Ricardo Villa's goal for Tottenham in the 1981 FA Cup Final replay and Archie Gemmill's goal for Scotland against Holland in the 1978 World Cup finals. More recently, Ariel Ortega's dribbling skills lit up Argentina's campaign in the 1998 World Cup finals.
However, dribbling is difficult to accomplish because of the sophistication of modern defences. Also it is a slow way to beat defenders to gain territorial advantage and runs a high risk of losing possession. Because of this it is a dying art.

On the other hand, Crooks will admit that the crowd is one of the factors involved in creating a psychological advantage when teams play at home. This is because, at the top level, things can be so finely balanced that every little advantage is important. Every, little advantage. The quality and state of the pitch, for example. It is not uncommon for devious managers virtually to flood their pitch, to make it difficult for passing sides to play their normal game. Other managers have legally widened – or narrowed – the pitch to suit their team's playing styles. It is rumoured that managers have sanded the areas near the corner posts, so that when long balls were played into those areas, the ball would hold up better.

Psychological advantages can come in the strangest of guises. In the 1981 FA Cup final, the Spurs players had convinced themselves that Manchester City's Dennis Tueart was the threat, the man for the big occasion. They were not even sure whether they were right to think so, other than the fact that he'd done it before in big games, and they feared he could do it again. When John Bond didn't pick Tueart for the final, or the replay, it gave the Spurs players a massive boost. And when Bond did finally bring on Tueart as a substitute in the replay, the Spurs team stepped back and suddenly a yard of space appeared that hadn't been there in the rest of the match.

Of course, if Bond had known this, he might well have played Tueart in the first place and Manchester City might have won their fifth FA Cup. But then he probably never asked himself what the Spurs players feared. Managers rarely do, they spend enough of their time dealing with their own demons. Concerning themselves with the psychological turmoils of players – theirs or

Headed goal

You will see many forwards attempting to head the ball down on to the opposing goal-line. This is often a harder shot for a goalkeeper to save, because of the bounce, than the header that remains in the air. Pele was a past master at it, and Gordon Banks' save of such a header in the 1970 World Cup finals is frequently cited as the 'save of the century'.

the opposition's – is a low priority in the scheme of things. But, by their very nature, footballers trade on their confidence. And this can be more fragile than it might outwardly appear. Slumps in form, particularly for goalscorers, can become a self-fulfilling spiral of despondency. The travails of the gifted Matthew Le Tissier became so great that the Southampton forward had to turn to a sports psychologist to try to rectify his erratic form.

The uncertainties surrounding the profession fuel a special kind of paranoia. All managers are chillingly familiar with the game's gallows-humour maxim about their job: 'the only certainty is the sack.' Their players feel much the same, except that they are less in charge of their destiny. A number of managers, like Cruyff with Lineker at Barcelona, are so rigid in forcing players to play the way they want them to play that they deny the player any expression of their natural ability. If you ever wonder why a club suddenly – and seemingly inexplicably – sells one of their more gifted, and crowd-pleasing, players, this conflict will probably be at the heart of it.

The crunch confrontation between manager and player would go something like this: 'Will you rely less on your ability for the good of the team, in order to win matches, the way *I want* to win matches?' The answer will invariably be: 'No.' Exit one highly-talented, gifted – but too expressive – player. The manager's motivation for this kind of authoritarianism does not simply stem from his character, but his conviction that if things are done his way, he'll still be in a job after the next match. That's his paranoia.

The player has a different view, but a similar paranoia. After all, he has a career to worry about as well. His. He didn't become a professional to

Substitutes

A substitute was first permitted in the 1965–6 season, and then only for injured players. Inevitably the 'injury rate' dramatically increased that season, as managers began to appreciate the value of tactical substitutions. The authorities realised the rule was unworkable and, at the start of the following season, a subsitution could be made for any reason. Over the years the numbers were gradually increased and now, in the Premiership, teams are allowed three substitutions from a panel of five.

play that way; he may not be any good at it; and why shouldn't he use the talent God blessed him with? This tension between the collective good (as perceived by the manager) and individual expression will always exist in a team game and, as modern football becomes more and more intense with its growing commercialisation, it will probably become more acute.

It's almost certainly impossible that any player today could cut through this Gordian knot the way George Best did in 1966. Manchester United were playing the second leg of a European Cup quarter-final against Benfica in Portugal and defending a slender one-goal lead. Matt Busby instructed the team to contain the Portuguese side for the first twenty minutes and not attack. The teenage Best nodded throughout the team talk, went out on the pitch and scored two goals in the first twelve minutes. United won 5–1. The home crowd mobbed Best.

But that was Best, today's managers would say. That's football, would be the players' riposte.

The Stuff of Dreams

Blackburn Rovers 1994–5

'You can learn from the past, but you shouldn't live in the past.'

Sir John Hall, chairman of Newcastle, March 1995

Blackburn Rovers. For me, those two words are two of the most comforting in football. I say this as a disinterested party. I am not a Blackburn fan, do not hail from Lancashire and paid Rovers scant attention until Kenny Dalglish became their manager in 1991. Then we all had to sit up and pay attention. Jack Walker, a multimillionaire local businessman and a lifelong fan, was pumping tens of millions into the club. For Dalglish to buy the best players, for an expensive new stand, for the future. Before Dalglish, Blackburn's tale was the run-of-the-mill story of a once great club whose initial euphoric success was followed by mind-numbing, soul-draining, interminable decline, as the world passed it by. Then, as if by magic, the dead weight of history was overturned by a philanthropic fan.

In his own way Walker did what we all secretly would wish to do, or at least hope somebody else would do, for our club. For it is the irrational – and usually quite unsustainable – belief that one day your club will be the best in the land that feeds our passion for the game. However in this instance, it happened. The dream came true. So forget the Manchester Uniteds, the Arsenals, the Liverpools for a moment, they always get their day in the sun. Let's share the Blackburn experience. But first we have to start at the beginning.

The things they say ...

'Bloody ridiculous. Can't we play them again tomorrow?'
Wilf Mannion on England's upset 1–0 defeat by the USA in the 1950 World Cup finals

'Some people called me a visionary, others a reactionary, while a few called me awkward or stubborn.'
Matt Busby, legendary Manchester United manager

'Our tactics are to equalise before the other side scores.'
Danny Blanchflower on Northern Ireland's strategy in the 1958 World Cup finals

As every schoolboy should know, the Football League was formed on 17 April 1888 at the Royal Hotel in Manchester. There were twelve founding members, half of whom were from Lancashire, the heartland of professional football, with Blackburn Rovers a leading light. It was a mould-breaking meeting at which the Liverpools, the Arsenals and the Uniteds didn't even bother to turn up, yet it still spawned the oldest League in the world. Of course, in those days, the biggest competition – in fact the only competition – was the FA Cup, and Blackburn had already carved their initials in history by winning it three times in a row before the birth of the Football League, in 1884, 1885 and 1886. For good measure they won it again in 1890 and 1891. So in those giddy, twilight days of Victorian England, we can safely say that Blackburn were the monarchs of football's aristocracy.

Indeed, Preston North End, who in 1889 became the first team to win the Double of FA Cup and League championship, had been established in 1881, six years after Blackburn were founded, with the express intention of outgunning their Lancashire rivals. To this end Major William Suddell, Preston's eminence grise, wheeled and dealed in the Scottish black market and campaigned for open professionalism inside the amateur-based Football Association. The conflict between the League and the FA, disagreements about money, and the underhand way success on the field of play was achieved are issues that still haunt the game today.

The League was an instant smash hit and quickly expanded beyond the original twelve founding fathers, as football took its rightful place as the

'Football is not really about winning, or goals, or saves, or supporters – it's about glory. It's about doing things in style, doing them with a flourish; it's about going out to beat the other lot, not waiting for them to die of boredom; it's about dreaming of the glory that the Double brought.'
Danny Blanchflower, captain of the Spurs side that won the Double in 1961

'England will win the World Cup.'
Alf Ramsey, on being appointed England manager in 1963

'You've beaten them once. Now you've got to do it again. Look at them! They're finished.'
Alf Ramsey's pep-talk on the pitch at Wembley before extra time in the 1966 World Cup final

national sport. Suddenly the game took shape. By the turn of the century, the names on the trophies began to have a ring familiar to us nearly a century later. Liverpool, champions for the first time in 1901. Tottenham, FA Cup winners for the first time in 1901. Manchester United, champions for the first time in 1908, Cup winners for the first time in 1909.

Blackburn peaked just before the First World War, winning the League championship twice, in 1912 and 1914. And in 1928, as Everton's Dixie Dean blasted himself into the record books with sixty goals, Rovers won the FA Cup for the sixth time, beating Huddersfield 3–1 at Wembley. But that was it, really. For the next half-century, the pride of Lancashire quietly slipped into that half world of relegation and promotion between the First and Second Division. In the 1970s they had even suffered the ignominy of two spells in the Third Division. More dishearteningly, as Rovers' fortunes waned, some of their neighbouring clubs, notably Manchester United and Liverpool, had grown into mega, super successful outfits and even the most diehard Rovers fan could not realistically kid himself that Rovers would ever be able to challenge those giants. This was particularly brought home in the 1980s when, season after season, they battled for promotion to then First Division only to fall at the final hurdle, reinforcing their modern status as also-rans. Nostalgia was the only comfort on the cold, crumbling terraces of rust-encrusted Ewood Park.

The tide of history certainly had not flowed in Blackburn's favour. The cotton industry that had been the lifeblood of Lancashire had declined to the point of extinction and the strength of the industrial north was now nothing more than a

'You'll be an immortal.'
Bill Shankly to Jock Stein, after Celtic won the European Cup in 1967

'The best place to defend is in the other side's penalty box.'
Jock Stein

'It was as if the janitor had gone to buy a tin of paint and come back with a Velasquez.'
David Lacey, in the *Guardian*, on Tottenham's coup of signing Ardiles and Villa

'We are the best in the world. We have beaten England, Lord Nelson, Sir Winston Churchill, Sir Anthony Eden, Clement Attlee, Henry Cooper, Lady Diana. We have beaten them all. Maggie Thatcher, can you hear me? Maggie Thatcher, your boys took a hell of a beating.'
Norwegian radio commentator on Norway's 2–1 victory over England in 1981

memory. Modern Britain bore little, if any, resemblance to the world that existed when Rovers drew 5–5 with Accrington Stanley in their first League match in September 1888. So different, in fact, that Accrington Stanley, one of the twelve original members, had fallen on hard times and had to resign from the League in 1962. While Blackburn Rovers slumbered in their time warp, momentous events came and went. In 1960, Blackburn briefly awoke from its slumbers, reaching the Cup final only to be thrashed 3–0 by Wolves and then dozed off for another generation or so, before their *annus mirabilis* in 1995.

To those unromantics who sagely say that the Rovers experience is an exception, and that an exception proves the rule, I would point to a strikingly similar exception in the corner of north-west Spain: Deportivo La Coruña, who, coincidentally, also play in blue-and-white. In 1988, just as Walker was pumping his first cash injection into Rovers, a Coruña businessman and politician, Cesar Augusto Lendoiro, became the president of Deportivo, a mid-table Second Division side who had spent more time there than in the First. He lured Arsenio Iglesias, a former Deportivo player and wily manager, out of retirement to pilot them back to the First Division. Then Lendoiro spent heavily in the transfer market. His acquisition of the two Brazilian internationals, Maura Silva and Bebeto, sent shock waves through Spain. Upstarts buying world-class players? Unthinkable. By 1995, SuperDepor (as the press dubbed them) had finished third, second and second in the League.

Admittedly wealth in itself is no guarantee of success (it took Manchester United over twenty-

'I just want to get through this trip without being quoted.'
Brian Clough

'I might go to Alcoholics Anonymous, but I think it'd be difficult for me to remain anonymous.'
George Best

'Football hooligans? Well, there are ninety-two club chairmen for a start.'
Brian Clough

'He was dynamic. If you lost a game, you lost to rubbish. If you won you had beaten a great team.'
Roger Hunt on the late Bill Shankly, the former Liverpool manager

'I've always said there's a place for the press, but they haven't dug it yet.'
Tommy Docherty

five years to finally 'buy' the championship), but it certainly helps. As does luck. Professional gamblers play on their skill, but they also know they still need the run of the cards to succeed. When, in 1992, Dalglish finally broke Blackburn's cycle of just missing out on promotion, they had scraped into the play-offs by finishing sixth, squeezed past Derby 5–4 on aggregate and won the final with a dubious Mike Newell penalty. Lucky man, our Kenny. As was our Brian. In 1977 Brian Clough took struggling Nottingham Forest out of the Second Division by narrowly finishing in third place. A year later they had won the League for the first time. Twelve months after that Forest were European champions. In between times, Clough broke the British transfer record by paying £1 million for Trevor Francis. Kenny Dalglish was hoping for the same sort of breaks at Blackburn, and like Clough he had shown he was prepared to spend heavily, breaking transfer records when necessary.

Persuading Dalglish to take over the helm at Rovers, seven months after he suddenly quit Liverpool complaining of 'pressure' was the shrewdest move Walker made. The pair appear to have had much in common: both rarely give interviews, preferring to keep the media at arm's length and both are tough, unsentimental, almost dour characters. In fact, the only streak of sentiment Walker has ever shown in his life was to bankroll the resurrection of Rovers. From a purely commercial point of view the £25 million spent on players was a massive gamble that would have had the financiers in the City shaking their heads. Having said that, Dalglish spent Walker's money wisely and well. When he broke the British transfer record and bought Alan Shearer in 1992

'Playing with wingers is more effective against European sides like Brazil than English sides like Wales.'
Ron Greenwood, then the England manager.

'My line isn't on the job.'
Ron Greenwood, then the England manager

'I would have given my right arm to have been a concert pianist.'
Bobby Robson

'Norman Whiteside's not only a good player, but he's spiteful in the nicest sense of the word.'
Ron Atkinson

'Alcoholism v Communism.'
Banner at Scotland v Soviet Union

for £3.6 million, some said he was crazy. They were wrong. Much the same happened two years later when Dalglish broke the record again, paying £5.5 million for Chris Sutton. Once again Dalglish's detractors were wide of the mark.

It quickly became apparent that Shearer was value for money with forty-seven priceless goals in his first sixty-one appearances. It was even more apparent when Kevin Keegan broke the world transfer record by paying £15 million to bring Shearer to Newcastle in 1996. (It was a curious twist of fate that reunited Dalglish and Shearer at Newcastle. Dalglish had surprised everybody by stepping down after Blackburn and then 'retiring'. Keegan's abrupt departure from Newcastle in 1997 was even more astonishing. That Dalglish once again entered the managerial fray did not register so highly on football's Richter scale.)

Of course, in Blackburn, Kenny could never have done anything wrong. In an affectionate and incisive piece in the *Independent*, Jim White painted a vivid picture of how the club's success lifted the whole town. According to Malcolm Doherty, the Labour leader of the council: 'There's no doubt that Rovers' success has put a spring in the step of the folk of this town. Lots of older people say not only it's the best team they've ever seen, but it's the best time they can remember. They just thought it would never happen.'

When White went to a match at Ewood he got the impression that 'it looked as if the whole town was turning out to watch Rovers, which with a population of 130,000 and an attendance of 28,000 is not far from the truth'. He also told a delightful little story that would warm any football-lover's

'There have been more mistakes in the manager's office than on the field. Players we have bought have not lived up to their reputations; youngsters have been introduced to the side too quickly; we have sold two full-backs without replacing them – and so on. But I have not lost confidence in myself one iota.'
Brian Clough, Forest manager

'When you've been thrown out of clubs like Barrow and Southport, you learn to live with disappointment.'
Peter Withe on being dropped by England

'Being given chances and not taking them, that's what life is all about.'
Ron Greenwood

heart. A Manchester United friend of his was attacked outside the ground by a band of young Rovers supporters and hit over the head with a bottle. As he fell, a group of older Rovers fans raced across the road. 'Stop that, Steven, we'll have none of that here', shouted one man. And then: 'Right Lee, I know your dad and I'm telephoning him when I get home.' They then apologised to the victim and offered to escort him back to his car.

Not that one anecdote proves that we have seen the back of hooliganism. Far from it. But it does suggest that a club that is closer to its fans and rewards them with magnificent facilities and a magnificent team might be rewarded with a more responsible set of supporters. In Blackburn, the club and the town were synonymous with failure and decline. Now that one half of the equation has been reversed, the inhabitants, almost naively, believe that the other half will change with it. As one season-ticket holder told White: 'I tell you how much it's got us going, women worry about the results. My mother, my wife want to come to the match, that's how much.'

It's totally obvious, but little remarked upon, that virtually all football clubs are named after a place. The very big clubs draw support from much wider afield than smaller clubs like Blackburn, and the likes of Manchester United in Britain and Barcelona in Spain are in effect national institutions. But that is very much a modern phenomenon, largely brought about by the all-pervasive influence of television and the dramatic increase in car ownership. The tradition of football-watching, and football-supporting, stretches back over a century and its roots lie in an identification with a place, a town or a locality in which you lived and worked,

'We looked bright all week in training, but the problem with football is that Saturday always comes along.'
Keith Burkinshaw, then Spurs manager

'The best team always wins. The rest is only gossip.'
Jimmy Sirrell, Notts County manager

'I just opened the trophy cabinet. Two Japanese prisoners of war came out.'
Tommy Docherty, then the Wolves manager

'Team spirit is an illusion you only glimpse when you win.'
Steve Archibald, then with Barcelona

got married, had kids and died. Your town, your club, your life. This isn't only true of football, the same applies to other sports as well. Rugby league, another game with its roots embedded in the industrial north of the nineteenth century, is one that immediately springs to mind. So when Rupert Murdoch was hi-jacking the English game and turning it into a Super League with enforced mergers where two or three clubs with 100–year histories would be blurred into each other, it was this passionate defence of place, of self-identification that forced rugby league into a quick rethink.

The argument was most cogently put by Simon Kelner, then the sports editor of the *Independent on Sunday*, where he explained that practically the only reason Featherstone, population 15,000, still exists is their rugby league team, 'Fev'. And their existence is predicated on the survival of Castleford, 'Cas', a few miles down the road. Without the bitter rivalry between the two, Featherstone, no more than a hamlet, would be as significant as, say, Knottingly. (Apologies to Knottingly readers. I know you are geographically nearer to Castleford than Featherstone, but that's my point.)

Back in the 1960s the American social psychologist, Irving Maslow identified a 'hierarchy of human needs' by which individuals or social groups aspire to higher levels of achievement as each level of need is satisfied. Thus, basic survival is of all-consuming interest to those under threat or in poverty, while social needs will become important to those with more security. Once all the lower levels of human need are satisfied, people aspire to the pinnacle of Maslow's hierarchy: 'self-actualisation', i.e. being who you want to be. If we applied this theory to

'I'd rather have a guy take me to a football match and have a drink afterwards than go to bed with someone.'
Samantha Fox, Page Three girl

'He gets great elevation on his balls.'
David Pleat on Diego Maradona

'Conjugate the verb "done great". I done great. He done great. We done great. They done great. The boy Lineker done great.'
Letter in the *Guardian*

'You might as well talk to my [six-week old] daughter. You'll get more sense out her.'
Kenny Dalglish, then the Liverpool manager, on Alex Ferguson's outbursts to the press

'I have told my players never to believe what I say about them in the papers.'
Graham Taylor, then the Aston Villa manager

'Football is irrelevant now, nobody is even asking after the other scores.'
Kenny Dalglish, the then Liverpool manager, immediately after the Hillsborough disaster

sport, we could deduce that supporting your club meets a much higher level of human need than might be imagined by those who simply see it as a form of mass regression to childhood or primitivism. Fans at least satisfy their social needs, even if they don't find self-realisation, in following their team. They might not like the jargon, but I bet the population of Blackburn would agree with the general proposition.

The reason I find the Blackburn Rovers story so interesting is that they have waited since 1914 for a League title, and since 1928 for a FA Cup victory. This is a town with serious patience and forbearance. In England, every club falls into decline at some stage in their history. But this doesn't necessarily mean they are dead and buried. Resurrections are possible. You just have to keep the faith.

Alan Shearer and Jack Walker with the Premiership trophy in 1995

In other countries, leading clubs exercise a hegemony unknown to English football, and thus their followers enjoy almost continuous success. Failure for them is often simply failing to win the championship, not relegation. But, unlike Scotland, Spain and Italy, for example, England has not had an elite set of sides that have consistently monopolised all the trophies. Instead there has been an ebb and flow with even the most successful sides all experiencing long, and dispiriting, fallow periods. The following list makes the point eloquently.

The top four:

Liverpool
(eighteen championships, five FA Cups)
didn't win a thing between 1947 and 1964, languished in the Second Division for eight seasons.

Manchester United
(eleven championships, nine FA Cups)
ditto between 1911 and 1948 and spent nine of those seasons in the Second Division.

Arsenal
(eleven championships, seven FA Cups)
slumbered in the First Division from 1953 to 1971.

Aston Villa
(seven championships, seven FA Cups)
went into hibernation between 1957 and 1981, even sinking so low as to spend two seasons in the Third Division and eight in the Second.

(By contrast Rangers have never finished lower than sixth in the Scottish League.)

What distinguishes these clubs (and there are many

'Penalty shoot-outs have nothing to do with football. It's like shooting poor wee ducks at a fairground.'
Aberdeen manager, Alex Smith, after his team won the Scottish Cup after 20 penalties

'It's difficult dealing with Mr Flashman because if you speak your mind, he tends to sack you.'
Edwin Stein, Barnet's assistant manager, sacked three times by the chairman. The manager, Barry Fry, was sacked eight times

'Hump it, bump it, whack it, might be one possible recipe for a good sex life, but it won't win us the World Cup.'
Ken Bates, Chelsea chairman

'When the seagulls follow a trawler it is because they think sardines will be thrown into the sea.'
Eric Cantona

'I have never, and will never, find any difference between the pass from Pele to Carlos Alberto in the final of the 1970 World Cup and the poetry of the young Rimbaud who stretches "cords from steeple to steeple and garlands from window to window".'
Eric Cantona

'I would pay to watch Cantona.'
George Best

'You can't win anything with kids.'
Alan Hansen on Alex Ferguson's Manchester United Babes

others, including Newcastle and Tottenham, to name but two) is not only that they all came back to recapture former glories, but that they had the resilience to do so. That strength derived not from their management, board of directors or their playing staff, it came from the soul of the club: the supporters who followed their club through thick and thin. Who else sustained them through the bad times? If you want the bottom line, who paid for the years of failure? The fans. It was the money that came through the turnstiles that was the lifeblood of the clubs. This is just one of the reasons why football is called the people's game.

Blackburn Rovers are a shining example of a club kept alive by its demotic following. The fact that Jack Walker, a long-suffering fan with deep pockets, provided the means does not in any way negate another fact: Rovers dug deep into their past, to where the English professional game was forged, and made it work, again. It just took a little longer than the Liverpools, Uniteds and Arsenals to get back on track. In the late twentieth century, money had to shout. Football was enjoying a well-deserved boom. Enter Blackburn Rovers, the underdogs of the twentieth century, who pipped Manchester United for the 1995 championship by a single point.

It Takes a Second to Win it All

Liverpool v Arsenal
Anfield, 26 May 1989

For only the second time in the 101-year history of the Football League, the championship was to be decided in the last game of the season between the teams occupying first and second position in the table. However the drama of the finale was overshadowed by the terrible loss of lives at the FA Cup semi-final. The tragedy of Hillsborough forty-one days earlier hung over football like a shroud. The shock of the deaths that day had rocked the sport to its very foundations.

Liverpool had soldiered on, with the blessing of the bereaved, and won an emotional FA Cup final in extra time against Everton and then beat West Ham 5-1 to set up the confrontation against Arsenal at Anfield. Arsenal themselves had accidentally contrived to keep the drama going to the very last match. In their previous two games – both at home – they had lost 2-1 to Derby and had drawn 2-2 with Wimbledon.

These results, coming on the back of a series of indifferent performances, meant that Arsenal had squandered the nineteen-point lead they had held over Liverpool in February. By contrast, Liverpool were unbeaten since New Year's day – twenty-four matches in total – and had not lost to Arsenal in four meetings that season (two draws and a win in the League Cup, and a draw in the League at Highbury). And

Arsenal had not won at Anfield since 1974. The omens for the north London club were not good.

The situation was clear-cut. If Arsenal did not beat Liverpool by two clear goals at Anfield then the title would go to the defending champions and Kenny Dalglish would become the first manager to have won the Double of FA Cup and League in the same season, twice. Unsurprisingly, the media billed it as 'The Match of the Century', with Liverpool the firm favourites.

The evening kick-off was put back by ten minutes because coachloads of Arsenal fans were delayed on the motorway. A number did not get into the ground until just before halftime. The Arsenal players, kitted out in a yellow strip to contrast with Liverpool's traditional red, gave bouquets of flowers to the crowd as a gesture of respect for those who had died at Hillsborough. To compound the historic occasion it was Sir Matt Busby's eightieth birthday: sadly, Don Revie, the former Leeds and England manager, died earlier that Friday.

The pundits were split as to which team had the psychological advantage. Liverpool could just decide to cling on, after all they hadn't lost by two goals at home since February 1986, over three years earlier, and that was to Everton. And derby matches are no respecters of form. Arsenal, however, had been averaging two goals away from home in their League matches that season. Before the match,

Bobby Robson, the then England manager, said: 'It's poised beautifully. Arsenal have to attack, which will provide opportunities for Liverpool. And if Arsenal score first ... then Liverpool will get more chances as Arsenal go for the second goal.'

Most people agreed with Robson's match predictions. But not George Graham, the Arsenal manager. In fact, his strategy was to do exactly the opposite of what was expected of him and his team. Instead of playing an obvious attacking formation, Graham opted for 5-3-1-1, a device that Arsenal had rarely used. There would be three centre-backs, David O'Leary, Tony Adams and Steve Bould. They would be flanked by two full-backs, Lee Dixon and Nigel Winterburn, who would operate almost as wingers. (With hindsight, this stratagem could be seen as the precursor of the 'wing-back' in English football.)

In midfield, Kevin Richardson, Michael Thomas and David Rocastle would seek to disturb the Liverpool style of neat, short passing. Alan Smith would operate upfront as the lone striker with Paul Merson as a split-striker behind him, a role he was used to, but, on this evening, playing that important bit deeper to help his three-man midfield battle with Liverpool's four-man midfield. On the bench, Graham had two attacking players, Perry Groves and Martin Hayes, in reserve.

Tactically, Graham was years ahead of his fellow managers that night. It took about half-a-decade for this formation to catch on in Britain – and then it was still largely seen as a defensive formation, a kind of sweeper system. But to employ a defensive formation in a match that you have to win by two clear goals? That was the beauty of it. Liverpool were the home side. And even though a 0–0 draw would have given Liverpool the title, it is in a footballer's blood that you have to attack when you are at home. Liverpool's players would have believed that they had no option but to attack. This played into Arsenal's hands.

The two full-backs, Dixon and Winterburn, were the key to Graham's strategy. They had to push up far enough on the wings in order to create extra problems for Liverpool's wide midfield players, notably John Barnes, who was seen as a major threat. Interestingly, eight years later, Arsenal, now managed by Arsène Wenger, employed virtually identical tactics with exactly the same players to outwit Manchester United.

Arsenal had gone 2–0 up at Highbury in November of 1997 only to let United equalise by halftime. Arsenal's problem was Ryan Giggs – he was just rampant. To win the game, win, Wenger took off a midfielder, Patrick Viera, who was injured, and brought on Bould, a defender, immediately after the break. The crowd despaired. They misunderstood what the coach was up to, thinking he was playing for the draw. Not at all. The very tactic that Graham had used so successfully at Anfield in 1989, was unleashed yet again. Three centre-backs with Dixon and Winterburn rampaging down the flanks. Giggs was nullified, substituted after twenty minutes, and Arsenal won 3–2.

Back to 1989. Liverpool lined up in the traditional 4–4–2 formation and immediately had problems. Arsenal's three-man midfield, could, at almost any point, become a six-man midfield with Merson and the two full-backs entering the fray. This was not the game the FA Cup-winners had anticipated. Traditionally, Liverpool rely on a very straightforward, and effective, style of play. They pass to the nearest red shirt, they keep it simple, they keep it quick. Arsenal would not let them do that and set out to break their rhythm of play by forcing them to contest the game in the cauldron of a highly-congested midfield.

Liverpool were also uncomfortable with the sweeper system that Arsenal were using. They just couldn't break it down. One of the ways to confound such a defensive formation is to play angled balls into the area that go away from the marker, leaving him in two minds as to what to do. Follow the ball? The man? Only once, in the entire match, did Liverpool play such a ball and it did create problems for the centre-backs.

Indeed, it was such a ball, albeit from a free-kick, that undid Liverpool's flat defence and prised the game open. After a tense, goalless first half, seven minutes after the break, Ronnie Whelan's foot was adjudged by the referee to be too high when he tussled with David Rocastle some thirty yards from Liverpool's goal. Winterburn's indirect free-kick was lofted towards the far post, on the blind-side of the defence, and Alan Smith timed his

Ray Houghton rises to challenge Arsenal's John Lukic under Anfield's floodlights during the epic game

darting run perfectly to break clear of a posse of red shirts just in front of the goal.

Not only was he onside, but he'd caught the entire defence, and the goalkeeper, Bruce Grobbelaar, on the hop. A glancing downward header that seemed to come more from his cheek than his forehead, bounced just over the line and up into the net, with Grobbelaar comprehensively beaten. The Liverpool players surrounded the referee in protest. At first it was thought they were suggesting that Smith had used his hand. (Television replays proved that he hadn't.) Then, the Liverpool bench claimed that the linesman had briefly raised his flag and then put it down again and that therefore Smith was offside. (Television replays proved that he wasn't.)

To his credit, given the huge importance of the result, the referee went to the linesman and discussed the incident for fully thirty seconds before awarding the goal. Now the game got really interesting. Who was in the driving seat? There were thirty-eight minutes left in the match; Arsenal had to score at least one more goal; a Liverpool goal would have required Arsenal to score twice more. How would you have played it?

Graham pushed Rocastle and Thomas further up to support Smith and Merson. Not quite stepping up a gear, but squeezing the space between midfield and Liverpool's goal up a notch and giving the Liverpool players yet another headache. Richardson and Thomas had already shown that they had the better of Whelan and McMahon in midfield. Arsenal's two wing-backs were coping with the rest, and Barnes was virtually non-existent. As was manager Dalglish's counter to Graham's canny tactics. Liverpool were on the back-foot. Not panicking, but mesmerised.

The Arsenal fans frenetically chanted: 'Attack! Attack!' The Liverpool players seemed content to sit on the 1–0 deficit, much as they had in the first half when the scores were dead even, at 0–0. In a sport where it is often said that 'attack is the best form of defence' it was surprising how few genuine chances of scoring Liverpool created in the ninety minutes.

Indeed, it was Arsenal who better understood the maxim in the latter stages of the second half and who, in the seventieth minute, came close to getting that crucial second goal. Richardson played a quick, neat ball into the penalty area and found Thomas, his fellow midfielder, unmarked near the penalty spot. Thomas stabbed the ball sharply with his right foot, but Grobbelaar just managed to get down to the shot. Twenty minutes later, Grobbelaar, and Liverpool, would not be so fortunate.

Seven minutes after Thomas's effort, Graham upped the stakes and rolled the

Michael Thomas (right) flicks the ball past Grobbelaar to win the League title in injury time

dice for the last time. Hayes had already replaced the tiring Merson, now Groves came on for Bould, his work done. Arsenal had taken off a defender, brought on an attacker and reverted to two centre-backs. The chase was on. But still Liverpool were in two minds: attack or massed defence? Whenever Arsenal went forward, Liverpool packed the penalty area with as many players as they could muster, even calling on Peter Beardsley (who had replaced the injured Ian Rush in the first half) and Barnes.

Every so often, Liverpool pressed forward in numbers in pursuit of the goal that would end their misery. In the eighty-second minute, John Aldridge hit a ball behind the defence that found Ray Houghton unmarked. It was one of Liverpool's best chances of the match. He scooped his shot over the bar. As the seconds ticked away, the entire Arsenal bench were waving to the team to tell them to get forward. With two minutes to go, and virtually the whole Arsenal team besieging the Liverpool goal, Beardsley broke away and bore down on goal, with Aldridge madly in pursuit.

As was Richardson. When Beardsley found Aldridge free on the edge of the box, Richardson's late, sliding effort from behind was enough to distract the striker and the goalkeeper Lukic was able to gather the tame shot easily. Richardson had to receive treatment on the pitch after his heroic effort and the drama was even further prolonged as the game was delayed. For the players on the pitch, and

the watching fans, it seemed like an
eternity. It was.

Ninety minutes had long gone. It was
time added on. Nobody – apart from the
referee – knew how long that was. A
minute? Two minutes? Three minutes?
Remember, it only takes a second to
score a goal, even in a match such us
this. It transpired that Brian Clough's
cliché should be re-written. The League
championship had been a ten-month
marathon beginning in August 1988, but
it was won in a second.

Dixon picked up the ball in the right-back
position, looked upfield and spotted Smith
in between the defence and midfield.
Dixon arced a long ball to the striker who,
in one movement, collected it and flicked
it forward into the path of the onrushing
Thomas.

Thomas's run from the heart of the
midfield had taken him straight into the
heart of Liverpool's defence. It was a
killing move. The ball bounced just right
for him as he skipped into the penalty
area and chipped the ball to his right over
the diving Grobbelaar. 2–0. Seventy
seconds later the final whistle blew.
Arsenal had won their ninth League title
and the Kop chanted: 'Boring, boring,
Arsenal.' I don't think so. Bloody clever,
bloody lucky Arsenal, would have been
more apt.

Kenny Dalglish was grudging in his praise
for Arsenal's achievement. 'They play in a
certain way which is not my way. We have

to give them a bit of credit, but we have to look at ourselves for the reasons we lost.' Precisely. Pretty, the game wasn't. There was too much at stake, the players were too hyped-up and the Arsenal tactics dominated the game. But dramatic? What more could you ask for? It was The Match of the Century.

The Arsenal team celebrate the championship after one of the most astonishing games in League history

'There are so many conservative forces in football that you cannot imagine. They want to stop anything new, but they cannot stop it. You must open this game. We cannot stay back in the last century. Our game is a game of the people and they are living with the rhythm of fast times where show business and entertainment matter. We must adapt.'
Sepp Blatter, March 1998

Sepp Blatter, a former amateur actor, has been castigated by his critics as a showman. But as general-secretary of the world's governing body he oversaw the most dramatic changes in the game since its invention and, although Fifa's titular head was for years its octogenarian president Joao Havelange, Blatter was the power behind the throne for well over a decade. Blatter is a moderniser, with a sense of tradition and, with that pedigree, in June 1998 assumed the throne when Havelange stepped down. So we should pay careful attention to his words.

Blatter, sixty-two years old in 1998, will be in charge of football until well into the first decade of the twenty-first century, when even more dramatic changes are in store. His heart is in the right place, but the abiding passion of many people in football is in a place proximate to the heart: that inside pocket in a grey suit that houses a wallet. Money has always affected the game; now it dominates it. To call this greed is to misunderstand the market forces that drive it. For a club to be successful in the modern era, they have to accumulate in order to speculate. This means that without untold fortunes, top clubs cannot buy the world's best players without paying undisclosed amounts of cash. Without the best players, they will not achieve the success they need to generate the income to continue that success by cornering the next crop of the best players.

That is the situation now. The future can only accelerate the process. Television is the prime motor force in this systematic market-led boom in football. And television is about audiences and advertising. Ratings bring in the advertising big bucks, which are the bottom line in TV. So, the deal between football and television is that football has to deliver the viewing figures or the cash cow dries up. Many see this is as a Faustian pact: football has sold its soul to the devil. I don't. Providing.

In 1997, the NFL renegotiated their television contracts and got *more* money for their product even though their ratings were *down*. Why? Because the television audience that American gridiron football delivered was exactly what the advertisers wanted. That's a different kind of bottom line. The kind of bottom line that Herr

Executive boxes over the Clock End at Highbury. Most large clubs now have similar facilities, and they are an important part of clubs' commercial operations. Ten years ago, they were unknown in British football

Blatter was talking about in the quote that heads this chapter. Young people; people with a significant disposable income; a definable market (75 per cent male); a fashionable crowd who like the heady mix of fast times, show business and entertainment. What's wrong with that? That's what football is largely about today and, having finally understood market capitalism, football is desperately trying to capitalise on its boom. The trick surely is: to have your cake and eat it. Sup with the devil, but sleep with the angels.

However. Television is a fickle bedfellow. Or to put it more bluntly, it is not a marriage, more an affair, with football as the more disposable partner. At the moment they both need each other. But television mostly has the upper hand. It already virtually decides when certain, important matches are played and when they kick off. Video recordings of games are now used in disciplinary hearings.

Television's power will inevitably grow because television companies are the paymasters, it's their (our) cash that fuels the game. Moreover, television permanently has a weapon up its sleeve that will always defy the Luddites that Blatter referred to: new technology and then newer technology. The question is not whether football will adapt to its changing circumstances, but *how*?

Football's biggest problem is to recognise that it is a nineteenth-century sport about to operate in the twenty-first century. This means grappling with six key issues: the fan base, the dwindling number of goals, recreational drugs and alcohol abuse, technology, the law, and the fat-cat clubs getting richer at the expense of the smaller clubs.

The Rising Cost of Football

On the face of it, everything is rosy in the garden of English football. Sky and the BBC are paying the Premier League £693 million for a four-year deal to televise their matches. By early 1998, eighteen English clubs had been floated on the stock exchange. In their 1997 annual report, the Premier League announced a turnover of £120 million – nearly double the previous year's. Attendances were up for the fourth year running and Premier League grounds were operating at 89 per cent capacity. However, increased turnover does not tell the whole picture. In 1997, the Premiership's pre-tax loss was £9.5 million, as football's increased revenue was largely spent on

The interior of Arsenal's World of Sport club shop, selling everything from branded keyrings to club strips. Over the past few years, strips have become the single biggest revenue earners for clubs' merchandising departments and something of a fashion statement for the fans

increased salaries for players and transfer fees while clubs desperately vied for on-the-field success. The television industry and paying supporters are both the beneficiaries and revenue-providers in this Catch-22.

The average annual cost of attending matches in 1998, according to a Premier League survey of nearly 30,000 supporters, was £758 including travel and tickets. It was even more expensive for Manchester United fans. They spent £1,248 to follow their club. On top of all that, football fans spent an average of £109 on club merchandising. Manchester United made £18.7 million in 1997 from merchandising alone. The money is clearly rolling in.

But there is a danger of killing the goose that lays the golden eggs as English football becomes more

The massive Manchester United Megastore at Old Trafford, by some way the largest club shop in Britain

bourgeois. Put bluntly, clubs are pricing themselves out of the range of their traditional fan base, the working class and teenagers. For the 1998–9 season, Chelsea's cheapest season ticket was £525 and its most expensive £1,250. It doesn't take a rocket scientist to realise that only the better-off can afford such prices. The short- and medium-term effect will be to increase revenue, but the long-term effect could be catastrophic. Privately, clubs admit that they realise that they have an ageing crowd, but they can't resist the easy cash. Manchester United, who could sell their 40,000 season tickets two-and-a-half times over with ease, are one club that are aware of the ageing problem but do not know what to do about it. Traditionally, football is a bug that you catch when you're young and you rarely get cured. But if teenagers can't actually go to matches, can't get their fortnightly fix, who's to say that the bug won't fade in time. Watching football on television is not the same thing. One of football's main strengths has always been its wide social base. The irony of the upsurge in interest in the game is that it is narrowing that base. What happens if the fashion changes, and the well-heeled turn their backs on football?

As a television spectacle, football games would be arid events without the atmosphere a raucous crowd provides. And, despite the huge revenue stream from television, the money generated at the gate is still the single most important entry on a club's annual accounts, somewhere between 40 per cent and 50 per cent. By gambling on the older, more middle-class customer and ever-increasing television money, football risks being squeezed on two fronts.

The Doomsday scenario goes something like this: football matches become ever more sterile as 1–0 results evolve into a succession of 0–0 draws as fear of failure causes defensive strategies to predominate; the middle classes become bored with the lack of action on the field and gradually fade away; the lack of atmosphere in the stadium, coupled with the poor fare, causes television audiences to go on the slide; advertisers start to drift away; the players' wage bill and the cost of transfers spirals out of control; the clubs, desperate to cover their costs, hike the price of tickets and lose even more paying customers. Television – which already provided 20 per cent of the Premiership's income in 1997 – gets cold feet about renewing contracts. If football were a real business, it would immediately go out of business at this point.

This scenario is not as fanciful as it sounds, and is extrapolated from the trends that exist in the game. Players' wages and the transfer market *are* out of control. The bill for players' wages in the 1996–7 season for the Premier League was £135 million; wages have increased 25 per cent each year for the six seasons since the Premiership's inception. And, in the 1995–6 season, £98 million disappeared out of the national game in transfer fees to non-English clubs. When Newcastle purchased Alan Shearer for an astronomical £15 million, at least the money stayed in the domestic game and could, theoretically, filter down to other English clubs via the transfer merry-go-round. But more worrying for English clubs is the role financiers take, now that football is trying to run itself as a business.

It is alleged that Kevin Keegan was forced to quit as Newcastle's manager because of their impending stock exchange flotation. Keegan was listed as an asset in Newcastle's application and, once he had indicated that he intended to resign at the end of the season, the application would have been seen as misleading if Keegan had still been included. So he had to go. Immediately. It made good business sense, never mind the impact on the team. When his successor, Kenny Dalglish, sold Les Ferdinand to Tottenham for £6 million he admitted that it was something he hadn't wanted to do. But the financiers decided that £6 million was too good to turn down for a thirty–year-old striker. Money talks, managers and players walk. Was it a coincidence that the Ferdinand transfer deal was struck just before Newcastle had to announce a loss of £23.6 million on the financial year? Dalglish has said the decision to sell Ferdinand was 'more a financial decision than a football decision'. And there are more financial decisions rather than football decisions in the pipeline.

The powers-that-be know all this. Graham Kelly, the FA's chief executive told the *Sunday Times*: 'Football is big business – perhaps the biggest change of all in recent times. Share flotations have given clubs the financial muscle to build new stadiums and bid for the world's best players. The downside is that in some cases the fans have felt distanced from their clubs. They feel their clubs are now owned by City institutions.'

This trend has serious momentum. One of Britain's richest men, Joe Lewis, whose total wealth is estimated at over £3 billion, has his fingers in at least four major European clubs and is on the lookout for more. The Bahamas-based Lewis personally owns 25 per cent of Rangers and, through the English National Investment Company, in which he has a 30 per cent stake, holds the majority shareholding in AEK Athens,

Vicenza and Slavia Prague. The other shareholders in ENIC are City investors – and even include Merseyside County Council's pension fund. Lewis is not a football fan. He is a businessman, pure and simple.

'We are looking to exploit pieces of intellectual property, and football has enormous value', Lewis told the *Guardian* in 1997. 'People have not yet realised how much it is worth. Once you've got a Manchester United fan, for instance, you have a captive client for life. You don't have that anywhere else, except perhaps in banking, and even there it's not the same.'

Chilling words. The potential flaw in Lewis's analysis of the economics of football – whether it is in Britain or Europe – is the blind loyalty of the fan. If that disappears, or declines, then the house of cards will come tumbling down. Television revenue, sponsorship, merchandising, ticket sales are all interconnected, and all vulnerable to the continuation of football's popularity.

Freedom of Movement

The full impact of the Bosman ruling – whereby players won the freedom of movement – has yet to be realised. As more and more foreign players move into European domestic Leagues, and earn fabulous wages, there is a strong danger of damaging the quality of the national sides of major European football powers like England, Italy and Spain, because fewer and fewer indigenous players will get the chance to play for the top clubs. (The money these three countries generate is probably the key factor in football's global economy.) Blatter believes this process has already started. 'The ruling was good for the players', he told *USA Today* in 1998, 'but bad for the local touch of the game. Take Italy. Practically all the key positions in the Italian League are occupied by foreigners, so when the Italian players get to the national squad they are not accustomed to playing in the key roles.' And weak national teams damage the overall credibility of the sport. The two booms in domestic football in England in the past thirty-odd years followed success by the national team in the World Cup: in 1966, when England won it, and 1990, when England reached the semi-final.

The Decline in Goals

Then there is the fare on offer. Each year, fewer and fewer goals are being scored as teams, and coaches, become more defensively-minded and more sophisticated in their spoiling tactics. If we take the post-Second World War World Cup finals as an index the trend is clear-cut.

In 1950, the average number of goals per match was 4.0; in 1970, 3.0; in 1990, 2.2 and in 1994, 2.7. The low-point was 2.2 goals per match in Italia 90. This was the cynical tournament of the penalty. The spotkick, either in a shoot-out, or during a match, epitomised the 1990 World Cup finals. It was a disgrace. In the final seven most important games – from the quarter-finals to the final – only two matches were decided by goals from open play. Four years later, Fifa's attempts to tilt the balance the other way in the 1994 tournament – by introducing three points for a win, outlawing the tackle from behind and liberally interpreting offside – favoured attacking play but only increased the frequency of goals by 0.5. And in Euro 96, where the 'Golden goal' was unveiled, the average goal yield was 1.97 a game. In thirty-one matches, there were five goalless draws, six 1–1 draws and six 1–0 victories. Boring.

To their credit, Fifa are continually trying to find ways to reverse this distressing trend. For the 1998 World Cup finals, the tackle from behind resulted in the player's dismissal and the interpretation of the offside rule was further relaxed. But this process will have to go even further if the most popular game on earth is going to stay that way. Without goals, there is no drama and the game descends into tedious sterility. Various suggestions were put forward: reduce the number of players; change the shape of the pitch; let matches be decided on the number of corners, and what have you. One wag even proposed that teams be forced to play with Scottish goalkeepers. Apart from being fanciful nonsense, the basic drawback to these notions is that they are not football.

One good idea mooted by Fifa to increase the number of goals scored was to experiment with altering the size of the actual goal. The dimensions of the goal – eight yards by eight feet – were decided by the Football Association in 1863 and 1865, and nobody knows why they chose that width and height. The minutes of the two meetings have no record of the reasoning behind the decisions. However, we can assume it had something to do with the size of the young, adult male population of mid-Victorian England. In those days, the average height of such males was just over 5ft 6ins. By the 1980s the average height had increased to over 5ft 10ins, a rise of 6 per cent. If we also take into account the dramatic improvements in muscularity, health, fitness and nutrition in the past 135 years, it seems reasonable to suggest that the size of the goal should be increased proportionally to reflect the difference between a nineteenth-century sport and a twenty-first-century one. Nine yards by nine feet would be a simple solution. And nobody would disagree that larger goals would inexorably lead to more goals. This suggestion has its precedents. Major League baseball is continually adjusting the height of the mound to keep the balance between the pitcher and batter roughly equal.

So what happened when Fifa put forward the modest proposal of trying out this experiment in some minor tournaments? The traditionalists came out of the woodwork and bleated to the media. Worse, British football journalists joined in with the moaning. 'You can't tinker with the game. It's worked for over a century, etc., etc.' was the essence of their argument. And the conservatives won. Fifa quietly dropped the idea, opting instead for continuing to change the guidelines given to referees to benefit attacking play, and thus, hopefully, maximise the number of goals scored. In the pervading climate, this was probably the best that Fifa could do, *politically*.

The Influence of the USA

But let's examine the thinking behind the opposition to Fifa's simple, radical proposal to open up the game by making it easier to score goals. One of the principal reasons, though not overtly stated, was that it would be a step towards Americanising the game. You don't believe it? First, more Europeans are USA-phobes than you would imagine: scratch them and they blame America for most of the ills of the world. Second, they hate the razzmatazz and glitter that Americans shower over their sports and fear that we will have to follow suit. Third, Fifa's stubborn decision to give the World Cup finals to America in 1994 clearly demonstrated what their long-term strategy was: to break into the one market they haven't conquered. This paranoia about the USA was further fuelled when Fifa floated the idea that the tournament in America would have four quarters, instead of two halves, to suit US TV and their advertisers. The idea quickly vanished as the European media waded in against it. However, the memory of Fifa's profane attempt to tamper with the sanctity of the game was not forgotten.

It is true that Fifa are hell-bent on making an impact on the American market, the one part of the world where football is not a major sport. It's the logic of capitalism: expand or wither. Blatter, in particular, is an advocate of developing the game Stateside. 'I do not understand how you look a gift horse in the mouth', he told *USA Today* in 1998. 'How is it that after such a well-organised World Cup in 1994 – the best ever – that the American market and television do not take greater advantage of this wonderful opportunity to promote the game?' The answers to that are many and complex, but if Fifa really believe that they can ever break the stranglehold that NBA basketball, NFL football and Major League baseball have on the psyche of the average American sports fan, they are kidding themselves.

Fifa sort of know this, but can't resist trying. As a world governing body, they would argue, they have to try to breach the final frontier. But invading America isn't at the top of their agenda. Avoiding the Doomsday scenario is. Which is why the interventions of their critics, whenever Fifa propose innovations, are so mischievous. It is always easier to argue that all changes will be for the worse. This is the 'if ain't broke, don't fix it' axiom – coined, incidentally, in America. Sadly, football *is* on the verge of being 'broke', and is in need of something more than an annual test to prove it is roadworthy. The opinion-formers would do the game a better service if they recognised this, contributed to the debate, and didn't just get their kicks out of carping about innovative changes whose sole purpose is to make the game more interesting to players and spectators. Remember, as you read this, that virtually every coach in the world is working like fury to produce teams that don't concede goals. The very logic of the modern game is potentially its own self-defeating nemesis.

Pressure on Players

This is also true of matters that do not take place on the football pitch and are another part of the problems that football has to confront as it boldly goes into the next century. Or not. Players are under more pressure than ever. From their clubs, from the spectators, from the media, from their own colleagues. Any error made on the football pitch is scrutinised in the most minute way by television and can came to haunt the player who committed it. The high-profile lifestyles of leading players are similarly scrutinised by the tabloid press. The demand for success, and the huge cost of failure, where relegation from the Premiership could threaten the very existence of the club, only increases the torment. With referees being forced to take harsher views of tackles, the number of bookings and suspensions has spiralled. The proliferation of fixtures and competitions takes its toll on the fitness and mental toughness of the players. The necessity of a squad system to cope the with injuries and suspensions inevitably

Under pressure. A pensive David Beckham, hero and villain of England's 1998 World Cup finals campaign

produces tensions in the dressing-room, as players constantly look over their shoulders and wonder how safe is their place in the team.

The plight of the superstar is a real one. This is how Manchester United's David Beckham explained it to *The Times* magazine: 'In my career everything has come so fast, it frightens me. I'm only twenty-two, sometimes people think I should be struggling more, but they don't understand that there's a lot of pressure at a club like this, plenty of younger kids coming through. You can't afford to have a bad game. I love the way of life up here in Manchester, but the way of life for a footballer – the money and so on – can be frightening at times.' He's not kidding. The top 400 players in England earn in excess of £6,000 a week. When Manchester United approached Juventus about acquiring Alessandro Del Piero they discovered that his annual wages would be £5 million. Arsenal's Dennis Bergkamp is said to be earning £25,000 a week.

These are young men, earning staggering amounts of money, who are likely to know little of life outside football. In a way, it's more surprising that so few have gone off the rails. Diego Maradona, of course, is the most extreme example of a player who went completely out of control and it's unlikely that there will many footballers capable of being tested positive for cocaine, accused of possessing the drug and distributing it, linked with a vice ring in Naples, arrested for cocaine when he fled back to Argentina to avoid prosecution, and then caught taking performance-enhancing drugs in the 1994 World Cup finals. After that he was arrested for firing on journalists lurking outside his home. But English football has already had its wake-up call about the damage the pressure can do to players. The England and Arsenal players, Paul Merson and Tony Adams, publicly confessed that they had turned to drink and had become alcoholics because of the pressure. Merson said he was also addicted to gambling and cocaine. That both players were treated sympathetically by their club and the FA, and that they had the strength of character to recover fully is gratifying, but should not lead to complacency.

As the pressure increases on players, they are going to use more and more expensive props to cope with it: alcohol, sex, gambling, drugs. This is a modern world that football administrators do not comprehend. Today, recreational drugs are endemic in our society and young men taking them is a commonplace social activity. The FA are gradually discovering this painful fact as more and more footballers are failing random drug tests for cocaine or cannabis, or both. If they added alcohol to their test, they would probably find even more testing positive, but then alcohol is not illegal. Suspending, or banning players, for indulging in recreational drug-taking seems misguided.

None of the players took those drugs to improve their performance. They weren't cheating, they were simply doing what hundreds of thousands of young males do on a weekend. It would be more useful, surely, to discover whether those players actually had a drug problem, and address the causes of it. Early diagnosis of a player heading for a breakdown is a better prescription than acting like outraged parents. Paul Merson's problem with booze couldn't have been plainer to spot. After he scored a goal he would mimic swigging pints of lager. On the pitch. Which, of course, was what he was up to every night down the boozer.

Why not Use the Technology Available?

Another major question that the football authorities will have to confront, sooner or later, is the role of technology – in particular, television replays of controversial incidents. It's another issue they have been ducking since TV became a serious force in live football. It is patently ridiculous that everybody with a television set knows that the referee got it wrong, but the decision can't be altered. A five-year-old child could explain this to Fifa, Uefa, the FA and every other football body that refuses to use the technology that already exists, never mind the technology to come.

The arguments against using instant replays during a game to correct a referee's mistake are interesting, but not persuasive. 'This is a human game based on human errors', Blatter told *USA Today*. 'If you take the error out of the game you take away an intrinsic part of the emotion, the passion and the humanity. It becomes a scientific thing.' In other words, to err is human, to get it right is dastardly science. But sports like athletics, swimming and horse racing use cameras routinely to determine the outcome of a race – and the world hasn't caved in. The defenders of the *status quo* argue that the advocates of going to an instant TV replay get to see the incident two or three times, and in slow motion, whereas the referee sees it once in real time. (Quite why this is an argument in favour of *not* using replays is, frankly, beyond me. But that's what they argue.) They also claim that overturning a referee's decision from a television studio would undermine his position as the arbiter on the field. They go on to say that things even themselves out over a season: one day it's for you, one day it's for them. They say that bad decisions are talking points of the game and part of its rich tapestry. And if you really used new technology to the full, eventually you'd have no referee on the pitch at all and that would turn football into a sterile computer game. And finally, tamper with the rules of the game at your peril. Devious coaches would find a way to use the new technology for a purpose for which it was not intended. They would manipulate it to their advantage.

For those in favour of using technology to prevent bad decisions affecting the outcome of matches, there is a glimmer of hope. A number of conservative

An example of the technology available today:
Nigel Winterburn of Arsenal dwarfed by one of the two Jumbotron screens at Highbury. These screens provide pre-match entertainment, replays and general team news and interviews.

opinion-formers are coming round to the idea that it should be used to verify whether a goal has actually been scored when there is some reasonable doubt, but that everything else should be left to the referee and his two assistants. This proposal would be akin to cricket's use of television to adjudicate on controversial run-outs. There could be a panel of two referees in a small TV studio in the stands who would review controversial goals. A time limit, of say 60 seconds, would be imposed while they re-play the incident on video. They could convey their decision electronically to touchline officials. If the replay was not clear-cut, then the original decision would stand. This softening of opinion started when the German and Portuguese football associations – to the anger of Uefa and Fifa – each ordered a football match to be replayed when television proved that a decisive goal wasn't a goal at all. Those precedents should logically lead to the conclusion that if the television evidence had been consulted at the time, the matches wouldn't have had to be replayed. And if television can be used after the event, why not at the time?

It is inevitable that instant replays will eventually be introduced. Given what could be at stake financially, one day a disgruntled and stubborn club will find a way of taking the football authorities to court over a blatant mistake and have the use of instant replay imposed on them. A club could argue that football authorities have a duty of care to ensure that justice is carried out during a game and, as they have the technology to do so, then they are being negligent in not using it. It was such a determined legal action by the Belgian footballer Jean-Marc Bosman that transformed the transfer market and gave professional footballers the normal rights of employees to ply their trade. It took Bosman nearly six years, and it had to go all the way to the European Court of Justice, but his persistence paid off, as Uefa discovered that football was not above European law. Bosman's lawyer, Jean Louis Dupont, has now become something of an expert in law and sport and is much sought after. Before Bosman and Dupont began their crusade, nobody in sport would have thought of taking their problems to Brussels; now there are hundreds of applications. Formula One motor racing has yet to learn whether or not it has breached Articles 85 and 86 of the Treaty of Rome by abusing its monopoly position. If the European Court decides it has, then that may well affect the status of every sport in Europe, including football. Then the crap will hit the fan-belt.

And, Finally ...

One thing you can't blame the football authorities for is the trend for rich clubs to get richer. In a capitalist economy, this is inevitable and unavoidable. It is an unfortunate fact of life in a market-led society that success that will be rewarded financially and that cash can be used to sustain that success, and so on, in a self-fulfilling cycle. However, it doesn't automatically follow that money can guarantee tangible rewards on the field of play. Barcelona and Real Madrid are two of the biggest and richest clubs in the world and yet, despite their untold wealth and their ambition to be the kings of Europe, Barcelona have only won the European Cup once, in 1992, and Real did not win it between 1966 and 1998. Manchester United went twenty-six years without winning the League title, from 1967 to 1993. And Manchester United's subsequent domestic successes were not simply down to splashing out on expensive players. Four or five other Premiership clubs spent more, but with not the same reward.

And, of course, there is Wimbledon. They have to operate on a shoestring, playing in somebody else's ground in front of crowds averaging around 15,000, but have stayed in the top flight ever since their arrival in the old First Division in 1986, winning the FA Cup in 1988.

There are steps the football authorities could take to try to level the playing field. They could take a leaf out of the NFL's book and impose a salary cap on each club and put a ceiling on the amount of money a club could spend in a season on buying new players. However, for this to work – and it does in America, the most capitalist-minded country on earth – it would have to be European-wide, otherwise clubs from those associations that have adopted such policies would be disadvantaged in European competitions. With players' wages spiralling out of control and transfer fees rocketing, it would make sound commercial sense for such measures to be introduced and go some way to changing the public perception that football is consumed by greed. However, it is probably wishful thinking to imagine that such an agreement could ever be struck, notwithstanding the restraint of trade implications that would be raised in Brussels.

The general picture I have painted of football's potential future prospects may seem unnecessarily bleak, but the trends are undeniable. It's a moot point whether anybody will pay any attention to the warning signs, although the appointment of a Football Task Force by the British government is a welcome initiative. Sadly, their task is formidable. The history of football is littered with examples of ignoring the obvious and blithely sticking heads in the sand. From England and the other three Home Countries boycotting the World

Cup for twenty years to the danger of stadium disasters such as Hillsborough being swept under the carpet. But despite all the gloom that can be predicted for the twenty-first century, football will, surely, muddle through and adapt to what is thrown in its path. Globally, the game is getting stronger, as the success of the emerging African nations amply demonstrates. Football is now commercially successful in Japan and, once again, there is a nascent professional league in America. Football has, after all, despite all the hiccups, cock-ups and dust-ups, for some reason or another, survived and thrived for nearly a century and a half. And no matter what the money-men think, ultimately, it is the people's game, and they will decide whether it has a future, or not. Tamper with them at your peril.

What follows is a selection and explanation of some of the words, phrases and clichés most commonly used by commentators and players.

Early doors

This commentator's classic describes the opening period of a game. It is usually used to emphasise the need to get off to a good start. For example, 'United really need to get a goal early doors.' This expression is thought to come from the now defunct custom whereby cinema admission was reduced to those customers who arrived early. Whatever its origin, there is no doubt that its arrival in the world of football comes courtesy of the self-styled king of football jargon Ron Atkinson.

Ricket (dropped a)

Defensive errors are embarrassing at best and at worst snatch defeat from the jaws of victory. Commentators and managers reserve the word 'ricket' for the most calamitous of defensive blunders. The classic ricket is the underhit backpass.

Technical player

Footballers are classically divided into two camps: industrious, hardworking players and enigmatic, skilful players. The second category are called many things, but the most bizarre is 'technical'. This description is thought to mean that such players have good technique.

Leading the line

A striker who works hard and is happy to receive the ball in difficult circumstances is often said to 'lead the line'. These players harry defenders, are willing runners and have the strength to receive the ball with their back to goal.

Hold your run

A good striker will avoid getting caught offside by timing his run so that he only ventures behind the last defender after the ball is played forward. This requires him to 'hold his run' until the last moment. Many strikers do this by making a diagonal run across the line of the defence.

Overlap

An overlap is a run made on the outside of a team-mate who is in possession of the ball. The overlapping player runs past the man with the ball, this either draws a defender toward him (and away from the ball), or puts him in a good position to receive a simple pass. The most common overlap is that made by a full-back coming past a winger.

Didn't see the incident

Footballers make terrible witnesses. From a sly, off-the-ball kick to a twenty-man brawl, you can guarantee that everybody questioned will utter the famous words, 'I didn't see the incident... honest, I really didn't see the incident.'

Dink

This is a popular word amongst players and TV commentators alike. It is used to describe a subtle, lofted pass over a defensive wall or an opponent.

Back door

A player who has his route to goal blocked by a defender will be pleased to hear a teammate's shout of 'back-door'. This call will tell him that his teammate is in a better position and that all he need do is pass the ball behind using a back-heel.

Committed

Commentators avoid describing players as dirty,

instead they call footballers with a penchant for fouling 'committed'. For the very top players words such as 'honest' and 'determined' are also used.

Professionalism

This is another favourite commentator's euphemism. 'Professionalism' describes cynical play which, though not technically against the rules, is against any spirit of sportsmanship.

Free transfer

A 'free transfer' is whereby a club allows a player to move to a new club without charging for the transfer of the player's registration. There is a great football myth that loyal players are given free transfers as reward for their service. This enables older players to negotiate more favourable personal terms as the new club do not have to pay a transfer fee. In reality clubs only ever grant free transfers to players who have little or no transfer value.

Nutmeg

One of the most embarrassing things to happen to a player on the field is falling victim to the dreaded 'nutmeg'. This is where the ball is played through the legs of a red-faced opponent. A successful nutmeg will always be confirmed by the obligatory shout of 'nuts' as the ball makes its way through the gate of the victim.

Squad player

All too often a euphemism for a player who will have left the club come the end of the season. This phrase is interchangeable with another description players fear: 'utility player'. A squad (or utility) player is not one of the manager's first choice players. He will start the season on the bench and be brought into the team to fill in for star players who are injured or suspended.

Cup-tied

The rules of most Cup competitions state that a player who has played a Cup match can only represent one club per season. A player who is transferred after playing in a Cup match for his old club cannot represent his new club in the same competition. He is said to be 'cup-tied' and is forced to sit out the Cup matches played that season by his new club.

Result

A manager will often be satisfied with a draw from fixtures in which his team is the underdog. In such situations it is common to say that the team 'got a result'. A draw from a difficult Cup game prevents elimination, and a League draw sees an addition to the points tally. This term is almost exclusively reserved for away teams, i.e. 'we came here and got a result'.

Absolutely/ Very much so

Post-match interviews with managers and players are rarely revealing or insightful. All too often the interviewer poses a rhetorical question… 'Your boys really did you proud out there today', to which the grateful interviewee provides a confirming response, 'absolutely… very much so.'

Professional foul

A cynical challenge whereby the sole intention is to prevent an opponent gaining an advantage, and where there is no possibility of making a fair tackle. A professional foul offers a calculated risk: making the challenge may result in a dismissal, but not making it may lead to a goal being conceded. The most famous professional foul was committed by Harald Schumacher, the West Germany keeper, against Patrick Battiston, France midfielder, in the semi-final of the 1982 World Cup. Schumacher rushed off his line to fell the onrushing Battiston, denying the Frenchman a goal-scoring opportunity and injuring him in the process. Schumacher's action went unpunished and West Germany won the game on penalties.

Hospital ball

A routine pass can become a painful prospect for the recipient if it is slightly misguided or underhit. All too often an opponent will be ready to pounce on such errors, and the receiver will be forced to get his body in the way of the challenge in order to retain possession. Injuries are the inevitable consequence ... the routine pass has become a 'hospital ball'.

Six-pointer

A crucial match between two teams competing for the same League goal – whether it be promotion, relegation, the Championship or European qualification – is described as a 'six-pointer'. A victory is the equivalent of two results going the way of the triumphant team, i.e. a win for themselves and a defeat for their rivals.

At the end of the day

Most footballers are fond of clichés, and a particular favourite is the phrase 'at the end of the day...' On most occasions this cliché is joined by a supplementary line, such as, 'the lads did a job,' or 'we're just taking it one game at a time', but Scotsman Brian McClair shocked journalists patiently awaiting the second barrel from the cliché shotgun when he sarcastically added '...it'll be 23.59.'

Their Cup final

Excuses are made early in football. So when a minnow plays a big fish, the game is inevitably billed as the smaller club's 'Cup final.' This statement works on two levels, it patronises the opposition and also explains away an embarrassing defeat, i.e. '... it's a question of motivation, they were up for it and we weren't ... it was their Cup final.'

Square

Square is an important word in the footballer's vocabulary. A defence which fails to adjust to a change in the opposition's attacking pattern, usually caused by a midfielder joining an attack, is said to be 'caught square'. A sideways pass to a team-mate is a 'square ball'.

Man on!

A player in possession of the ball relies on his team-mates to warn him if he is about to be tackled on his blindside. A shout of 'man on!' is the standard warning cry.

Midfield general

Midfield players are described in one of three ways: ball-winner, play-maker or midfield general. A ball-winner is a player who is industrious and works to regain possession for his team when it is lost. A play-maker is a midfielder who starts off attacking moves. These players are usually gifted passers of the ball, but rarely work hard when their team is not in possession. The midfield general is, typically, a player who combines the workrate of the ball-winner with the skill of the play-maker. This description is reserved for only the most accomplished midfielders.

Showboating

Any skilful play which provides no advantage, but merely pleases the crowd and humiliates the victim is described as 'showboating'.

Target man

A 'target man' is typically (though not necessarily) tall and strong. He has the strength to receive the ball with his back to goal, while surrounded by defenders, and the aerial ability to win any high balls which are played in his general direction. A good target man is always looking to receive the ball and helps his teammates by providing them with an outlet when they are under pressure.

Bosman

Any footballer playing in a European Union country is entitled to a free transfer to any club within the EU when his contract expires. This situation came about following a case taken to the European Court of Justice by Belgian footballer Jean-Marc Bosman. As a result, any footballer who moves clubs on this basis, is said to have been transferred on a 'Bosman'.

Give and go

An exchange of passes between two players is variously described as a 'one-two', a 'give-and-go' or a 'wall-pass'. This move, though simple, can be extremely effective as it requires defenders to be alert to an off-the-ball run. If the defender goes to sleep and follows the ball, the man making the run will be in the clear.

WORLD TEAM OF EMERGING STARS
(1–3–3–1–2)

Coach: Marcello Lippi (Juventus)

Alex Manninger (Arsenal, Austria)

Igor Tudor (Hadjuk Split, Croatia)

Alessandro Nesta (Lazio, Italy)

Rio Ferdinand (West Ham, England)

Winston Bogarde (Barcelona, Holland)

Lars Ricken (Borussia Dortmund, Germany)

Dejan Stankovic (Red Star Belgrade, Yugoslavia)

Denilson (Sao Paulo, Brazil)

Rivaldo (Barcelona, Brazil)

Marcelo Salas (River Plate, Chile)

Raul (Real Madrid, Spain)

Alex Manninger
A fearless, confident twenty-two-year-old who grasped his chance with both hands when David Seaman was injured for two months in 1998, keeping six clean sheets for Arsenal

Igor Tudor
A tall, highly-rated *libero* who has been avidly pursued by several Italian clubs. A young elegant player who delights in floating around at the back, he intercepts passes almost at will, and reads the game well

Alessandro Nesta
Scored the vital goal in the 1998 Italian Cup final
for Lazio. Replaced Ciro Ferrara as the right-sided
defender in the Italian national team. Cool-headed,
and consequently is frequently assigned to nullify
the opposition's key attacker

Rio Ferdinand
Inevitably, he is regarded at West Ham as the heir
to the late Bobby Moore. The antithesis of the
conventional English centre-back. He is comfortable
on the ball and likes to break out of defence

Rio Ferdinand

Winston Bogarde
Powerfully built with a strong left foot, he made
his name at Ajax and has thrived under ex-Ajax
boss Louis van Gaal at Barcelona after a
disappointing six months with Milan

Lars Ricken
Scored a brilliant goal in the 1997 European Cup final. A former under-21 star with the national side, he is the most talented youngster to have come out of Germany in recent years

Dejan Stankovic
The latest first-class product to fall off the conveyer-belt of Yugoslav talent. Scored twice on his international debut against South Korea in April 1998, shortly after agreeing to move to Lazio from Red Star Belgrade

Denilson
All left foot, but it never did Maradona any harm. The £21 million transfer of this highly-gifted prodigy to Spain's Real Betis after the 1998 World Cup finals made him the most expensive player in the world

Rivaldo
Another left-footed Brazilian with extraordinary technique, he is highly-regarded in Spain – pundits there claim he is better than Ronaldo – after two great seasons with Deportivo La Coruna and Barcelona, 1996–8

Marcelo Salas
A stocky South American striker and a regular scorer for Chile and River Plate. Was pursued by Manchester United but agreed to join Lazio for £12m the day after setting Wembley alight with two breathtaking goals against England in the build-up to the 1998 World Cup finals

Raul
The golden boy of Spanish football, a teenage sensation with Real Madrid, he scores and

creates goals with equal aptitude. Now a regular Spanish international

Coach: Marcello Lippi of Juventus. Has proved he has the character to handle, and mould, a team of international superstars and turn them into a formidable winning-machine week in, week out

Compiled by Mike Hammond and Chris Nawrat. Mike Hammond is the General Editor of the *European Football Yearbook.*

Rivaldo

The Organisations

Fifa. The world governing body, based in Zurich. Organises the World Cup tournament.
Tel No: 00 411 384 9595

Uefa. The European governing body, based in Nyon, Switzerland. Organises the European Champions League for Europe's elite clubs; the European Cup Winners Cup for the Cup-winners of all affiliated nations; the Uefa Cup for those clubs that fall just outside the elite and the European championships for national sides.
Tel No: 00 41 22 994 44 44

The FA. English football's governing body for the international arena, the Premiership and the amateur game. Also responsible for disciplinary purposes for the Football League. Organises the FA Cup.
Tel No: 0171 262 4542.

The Premiership. The body that runs the Premier League.
Tel No: 0171 262 4542

The Football League. The body that runs the three English Divisions. Organises the Football League Cup in which the Premiership clubs also compete. The winner has an automatic place in the Uefa Cup.
Tel No: 01253 729421

Professional Footballers' Association. The players' trade union.
Tel No: 0161 236 0575

The Football Supporters Association.
Tel No: 0151 709 2594

Although France won their first World Cup, the old guard of footballing nations still largely held sway. The final eight teams included four of the six countries that had won the previous fifteen tournaments – Argentina, Brazil, Italy and Germany – and Holland, twice losing finalists. So, despite Fifa increasing the number of finalists to thirty-two from the twenty-four that played in 1994, the emerging nations came to the party but were shown the door before the real festivities began in the second round. Before that we had seventeen days of virtually non-stop football which did nothing more than eliminate those teams that everybody knew were going to be on an early plane home anyway. The only surprises were the elimination of Spain and Bulgaria.

There are two principal objections to the thirty-two team format as it is currently constituted. First, forty-eight generally predictable matches dull the appetite for when the real thing happens. And, if Fifa wish to hang on to those new supporters who are attracted by a World Cup, they should not dish up poor fare. Second, this is supposed to be a World Cup, which should mean a tournament of the world's best and not simply a festival based purely on geography. Who could possibly justify, on football terms, the inclusion of Japan – which lost all three games and scored one goal – at the expense, say, of Portugal, one of Europe's stronger teams? The World Cup is sixty-eight years old and, before the advent of the jet plane, qualifying groups based on geography made sense then. But today?

Apart from the violence perpetrated by English and German hooligans, the tournament was very successful. France were worthy winners – although they did ride their luck in the weaker half of the draw – not losing any of their games and conceding only two goals, one of them a penalty. Their 3–0 defeat of the defending champions in the final was Brazil's worst defeat in their illustrious World Cup history.

The host nation's victory should not have come as a surprise. Brazil were eminently beatable – defeats by the USA and Argentina in the run-up to the tournament had demonstrated that – and this was one of the most open World Cups since 1982. Four of the other pre-tournament favourites, Argentina, England, Italy and Holland, all lost narrowly. Argentina were undone by a last-minute goal and the other three fell in penalty shoot-outs. Even Germany's 3–0 defeat at the hands of Croatia, who finished third, was only surprising because of the scale of the defeat.

That France ultimately triumphed with a mainly ineffective strike force says volumes about the trends in the game. A solid defence, a creative and combative midfield, versatile players – who can defend and score goals – this is the modern game. France, like most other teams in the tournament, played with wing-backs who, by attacking down the flanks, were able to give the game more width and reduce the congestion in midfield. However, this strategy puts a premium on pace as we witnessed match after match played in top gear. Gone was the slow-quick-quick-slow probing that countries such as Italy and Brazil used to employ. Now, everybody plays flat out. This requires the modern player to be a highly-charged athlete as well as possessing the skills to improvise in the hectic hurly-burly of a high-speed match. The likes of Zidane, Desailly, Owen and Ronaldo are the blue-print for the future.

The fear that Fifa's refereeing guidelines would lead to a rash of dubious red cards never really materialised and the dreaded penalty shoot-out only resolved three of the final sixteen matches, with one being settled by the even crueller 'Golden goal'. Most referees let the games flow and the crackdown on discipline helped the tournament maintain the same average number of goals per game, 2.7, as in America four years previously. Given the goal yield at Euro 96 was a paltry 1.97 a game, it bodes well for the future to see the trend reversed.

There have been many books published on football and so it is difficult to make a definitive selection of the ones really worth reading. However, the following ten books are my 'top ten'.

Association Football and English Society, 1863–1915, Tony Mason. Although a somewhat dry and academic work, this book provides fascinating insights into the formative years of English football.

European Football Yearbook. The 'bible' of European football and essential for those whose vision occasionally crosses the Channel.

Football Against the Enemy, Simon Kuper. A brilliant series of incisive essays about football around the globe.

Illustrated History of Football, Chris Nawrat and Steve Hutchings. A season-by-season chronicle interwoven with profiles, features and statistics. A reference book that is also a good read.

Only a Game, Eamon Dunphy. An honest professional's diary of the season. Takes you into the mind of a player.

Rothman's Football Yearbook (1970 onwards). The 'bible' of British football. Indispensable for any serious fan.

The Football Managers, Johnny Rogan. An absorbing analysis of the most successful post-war British managers from Matt Busby to Graham Taylor.

The Glory Game, Hunter Davies. A timeless, fascinating, fly-on-the-wall account of Tottenham's 1971–2 season. Tells the inside story of how a club – and its team – ticks.

The Guinness Record of the FA Cup, Mike Collett. A thorough and meticulously researched reference book on the game's oldest club competition.

The Story of the World Cup. Brian Glanville. The best history of the world's most important tournament.

Football supporters have an insatiable appetite for news about their club. All gossip, however ridiculous, is sought out, debated and then communicated to anybody who will listen. And the internet is the perfect source for footie news, some well-researched, much scurrilous.

Official Sites
Most League, and some non-League, clubs have their own official web sites. These vary in quality from professionally-produced, all-singing, all-dancing sites with video clips, pictures and match reports, to dull-looking text-based sites. Whatever the design and gizmos are like, the best sites are those that are quick to access, stable (i.e. don't continually crash your machine) and regularly updated.

Homepages and non-official sites
As well as official sites, there are hundreds of club-specific homepages and unofficial sites on the Web. A search site, for example Yahoo (www.yahoo.com), will help you locate the homepages in which you're interested. Each club usually has a long list of these unofficial sites and, though many are frustratingly difficult to access, occasionally you will stumble across one that is both well-maintained and well-written. Some of the best football internet sites are unofficial and are often associated with fanzines. The QPR fanzine, *A Kick Up The R's,* has a notable site (www.qpr.org/akutrs) and *The Everton Roundhouse* (evertonfc.merseyworld.com) is another unofficial site worth a visit.

Chris Nawrat has been a sports journalist, specialising in football, since 1979. He began at the *Morning Star* where he was Pools Forecaster of the Year in 1980 and covered the 1982 World Cup in Spain. Chris moved to the *Sunday Times* in the early 1980s and was the deputy sports editor from 1986 to 1988 and the sports editor from 1988 to 1994. In 1985 he was joint Sports Reporter of the Year for investigations into football and boxing.

Currently he is the sports editor of Channel 4's internet site at www.channel4.com/sport. His previous books include the *Illustrated History of Football* and the *Illustrated History of Twentieth Century Sport*. Chris is a lifelong Spurs supporter and has a minuscule shareholding in the club.

Inside**the**Game
THE ESSENTIAL GUIDE TO SPECTATOR SPORT

This new series is designed to provide a complete overview of the major world sports for the rapidly-expanding spectator market, covering the history, the rules, the main terms, how the sport is played, the great stars and teams, the sport today and the future.

Intelligently written by leading sports journalists, the books are aimed at the passionate but discerning new sports fan. They take an alternative perspective to other sports titles, going beyond the normally bland observations and reflections of the commentator and professional sportsperson, providing readers with an informed and cliché-free framework within which to understand and appreciate the great sporting dramas.

Titles currently available:

Inside the Game: **Cricket** by Rob Steen
ISBN 1 84046 031 8

Inside the Game: **Golf** by Derek Lawrenson
ISBN 1 84046 030 X

Inside the Game: **Football** by Chris Nawrat
ISBN 1 84046 028 8

Inside the Game: **Boxing** by Harry Mullan
ISBN 1 84046 029 6

Titles for 1999:

Rugby Union, Formula 1, Horse Racing.

INDEX